A Dual Path

Sacred Practices and Bodywork

By Monique Illona

To a Spirit Awakened

A Dual Path: Sacred Practices and Bodywork
By Monique Illona

First Edition, 2014

Sacred Bodywork, Dual Path Institute, and Hand in Hand Massage are federally trademarked.

Disclaimer:

The author of this book does not dispense medical advice nor prescribe the use of any technique for treatment of physical, emotional, or medical problems. The reader takes full responsibility for the application of wisdom within and their emotional, physical, and spiritual wellbeing. The book is sold for information purposes only; neither the author nor the publisher will be held accountable for the reader's actions, or of any said consequences.

Library of Congress Control Number (LCCN): 2013957918

ISBN # ISBN-10: 0989606201   ISBN-13: 978-0-9896062-0-2

Cover photography by Paula Muller

Design by Nancy Wolinski and Monique Illona

Dual Path Press

Marblehead, MA

Contents

Part 4: The Client and Professional Guide

Part 5: My Sacred Journey

Dedication

It is my belief that each of us is born

with a beautiful and sensitive nature,

but sadly, world events make us believe

this nature is dangerous, a weakness,

and we hide from it and bury it,

and laugh when we catch glimpses of it in each other.

We learn to harden ourselves, and develop strengths

and systems within ourselves to disguise it.

This hardening is a hardening and deadening of our spirit.

It can take a long time to nurture a spirit back to life,

but your sensitive nature remains intact,

a wondrous light at your core,

your source of strength and insight.

However, you are, and need to be, its protector,

holding your inner world

delicately in the palm of your hands.

May your hands always be full

and your spirit always shine bright.

— To you who holds this book in your hands, to all humankind

Foreword

The high point of western civilization was the building of Chartres Cathedral. Chartres embodied the fusion of art, craftsmanship, and spirituality with a dedication to work that is almost unknown today — thousands of artisans working and praying together, with little financial reward, to erect an edifice that celebrated the sacred, an edifice that many of them knew they would never see completed.

In the nineteenth century, when the Christian missionaries tried to convert the 'heathen' Comanche, they were singularly unsuccessful. No matter what they did to convince the Comanche to believe in something they could not see, the Holy Trinity, it made no sense to them. The Comanche saw God around them every day. Why have beliefs, when you have direct experience? The sacred was already part of their daily life.

We can bring the sacred into our daily life. This book is a guide to a latter-day continuation of the spiritual artisans' craft: the union of personal work (including meditation, prayer, reflection, and insight), with professional work, and the coupling of the two, so that we can bring the sacred into our daily work, not as a belief, but as direct personal experience. It is a tool box and guide to the environmentally conscious, sensitive individual, to empowering you to bring those things that are sacred to you, into the inter-personal world and the material world.

There comes a time when we realize that there is no lasting fulfillment in material possessions, that bigger is not better, and that having more is no guarantee that we will no longer feel alone, empty, or worthless. If we can find an inner work that nurtures our outer work, and an outer work that enriches our inner life, then we will have found our calling.

When you find the job you love, that is the last day you get up in the morning and go to work.

Monique Illona is a courageous woman who has devoted her life to making work sacred. It has been a long and difficult path for her, but her perseverance and authenticity, have borne fruit. Her work has become sacred; her life, fulfilled.

In this book, Monique shares her daily spiritual practices with the reader, and describes in detail how she has brought the results of almost thirty years of inner work into her daily life. She helps us understand how to 'gracefully develop' our skills and gifts, by explaining, with inspired choices, allegory and example, a system of personal preparation and inner work.

It is so important that we continue to pay attention to our journey, and ensure continued development in every vital area of our life. This book gives us important tools to do that; to keep us connected to our true selves and to each other, and to help keep us growing.

May the beauty you love, be what you do.

Hugh Milne, founder of the Milne Institute
Big Sur, California
July 2013

Part 1

A New Mindset

Welcome to Our Sacred Universe

We are sacred, each and every one of us.

The sacred is the seed at the core of our being and the potential of living a sacred life is available in every moment.

Unfortunately our moments can be clouded with thoughts, plans, memories, wounds, and responsibilities. This cloud creates, and is a manifestation of, a disruption in our energetic matrix.

This disruption in our energetic matrix may cause us to feel dissatisfied with our lives or with the world, angry at our circumstances, even ashamed of past or present actions or decisions. These feelings do not negate that *we are sacred*, they only inform us of a fundamental, but potentially temporary, disconnection from the sacred within.

With each step forward on this path we find ourselves increasingly present, with a more awakened spirit. As we journey on, and our energetic matrix begins to clear, the sacred moves from *concept*, to a living *experience of the sacred within*.

The province of the sacred is not only within us; once we connect to it, we are connected to the *universe* of the sacred, and by so doing we become its guardians.

The Dual Path is one towards guardianship of our own sacred beings and the sacred world we inhabit.

While the Sacred Practices in this book work towards clearing the matrix, Sacred Bodywork is an invocation of the sacred, allowing us to experience and honor this profound and transformational province.

To
an
Awakened
Spirit

The Story of Our Creation

As we come in to this world, on the day of our birth, we are each of us greeted with the full potential of what life has to offer. Just as quickly, we are each greeted with a family or societal structure and taught its rules and expectations. We learn or pick up attitudes, judgments, prejudices, and even how to hold and move our bodies, our tone of voice and sentence structure, and how to behave when we are angry, sad, happy, tired, hungry and upset.

However, natural and challenging this process is, it shapes and distorts the true nature of the energetic matrix we came into the world with.

The Script We Are Handed

Position

Who respects, listens to, trusts and obeys whom? Who is "top dog" and where does everyone else stand (father, mother, siblings, teachers)? What position do you hold, and how do you take this with you as you grow?

Gender

What is acceptable attire? How you can wear your hair, speak, walk, get sad and angry, who hangs up the laundry and who takes out the garbage?

Religion

What do we believe in? Where, how often, and in front of whom do we express our faith?

Politics and Affiliations

There is pressure to follow or choose everything from political parties to sports teams and friends.

Relationships and Sexual Preferences

We are given acceptable timelines and descriptions of a fitting partner, with rules around them being of the same age, gender, religion, politics and position.

Success

Measurements of success or a life well-lived are often marital status, children, house ownership, job and level of education and wealth. Internal measurements of success also include contentment, equanimity, stillness, love and health.

Roots Divorced from our Dreams

Our Earthly lives keep us occupied with right and wrong, decisions, choices, responsibilities, education, clothing styles, makeup, haircuts, dating, relationships, eating and drinking habits, life, death, news stories, work, paying bills, doing the dishes, our personal foibles, and the list goes on.

Our original nature and energetic matrix becomes distorted as we find ourselves divorced from any dreams or aspirations we once had. This process of loss creates a hardened shell of habit and repetition in which we tend to feel lost, saddened, scared, hurt, injured or armored, while deep inside we wait, want and strive to reconnect to the root of our spirit.

Many of us end our days wondering what meaning our lives have had, having lived by *searching* for meaning or *coping* with the lack of it (most often in religion, drugs, alcohol and relationships).

At any stage in our lives, as we step on the path to clearing our energetic matrix, meaning returns as our spirit, once again, awakens.

Spiraling Up to an Awakened Spirit

Under the challenging forces of our script, we can lose touch with the original core of our sacredness. When this happens, we can find ourselves in a downward spiral, a state of stagnation and increasing difficulty.

Our Energetic Matrix

Any physics professor will tell you that our entire universe is nothing but energy, including our bodies. Functional MRI's show that even our brains are made up of patterns and flows of energy. When we think of a healthy body we think in terms of nutrition and exercise but our system is an energetic matrix, a field of information that is constantly in flux and sensitive to the nuances of everyday life.

Disruptions in the Energetic Matrix

The health and integrity of this matrix can be easily disturbed or even disrupted by:

• Exposure to negative energy in the form of images, words, attitudes, behavior

• Difficult experiences

• Physical, emotional or other types of trauma

If we live our lives with the disruptions these cause, we spiral into a life of increasing difficulty, full of unhelpful and unhealthy behaviors, thoughts, emotional and physical patterns.

We respond to these disruptions in one of, or a combination of, the following ways:

- Anger
- Shame
- Guilt
- Depression
- Fear
- Dissatisfaction
- Loss of Self
- Denial

Unhealthy Coping Mechanisms

In turn these lead to any number of unhealthy coping mechanisms that often lead to:

- Unhealthy behavior, thought, emotional and physical patterns
- Illness

Changing Directions with the Dual Path

A Dual Path takes you through the steps necessary to spiral up to a life that is increasingly healthy and vibrant. As you proceed, you will discover that this path is not linear, the practices interweave through the following steps:

Realization

This book is in your hands because you have had a realization that you long to express your sacredness. You may also have wondered, Is this all there is?, or thought the life you have, the path you are on is unfulfilling, that you have not reached your potential or even that it is an unhealthy one.

Finding the Path Within

Many of us search for and connect to this path in yoga or meditation classes, in hobbies we have, by spending time in nature or houses of worship. We often move towards these activities because they light the fire of our spirit. Unfortunately we soon become advocates and followers of the activity rather than our spirit. A Dual Path is not in conflict with any other path your are on, it just leads you back to the origination point: the seed of the sacred that lies within. A Dual Path then nurtures this seed and helps it grow strong.

Choice

Just as we choose to step on the path, we also choose to step off. This Dual path consciously explores and diffuses the discomforts or resistance that is held in our energetic matrix that lead us astray. The clearing of our energetic matrix is what allows us to return to the path time and time again, until the time comes when we walk it without faltering.

An Unending Path

While we are all connected by the universal challenges of life, we are all greeted with what we think of as our own unique life challenges. Within our lifetime this path never ends, giving us unending opportunities for:

- Personal growth and self-transformation
- Clearing our energetic matrix
- Reawakening our spirit
- Creating a life that is sacred
- Forging a universal relationship based on compassion

The Dual Path

EARTH

Sacred Practices
Physical Body
Limitation
Low Vibrational Frequency
Opaque, Dense
Hard, Compact, Compressed, Heavy
Stillness
Movement (Cycles)
Grounding and Stability
Repetition
Habits
Effort
Mundane
Responsibilities, Expectations, Challenges
Client and Professional

HEAVEN

Sacred Bodywork
Subtle Body
Infinite Potential
High Vibrational Frequency
Transparent, Translucent
Soft, Open, Clear, Light
Movement
Stillness (Calm)
Letting Go
Exploration
Transformation
Ease
Sacred
Spirit, Dreams, Aspirations
Client and Professional

We live in the world of waking up and brushing our teeth, doing what we need to do and what is expected of us. We play out our patterns and habits on a stage, tied to stories of who we are and how we understand ourselves. Our shoes are well worn from traveling the Earthly path, struggling with its expectations and responsibilities while we try to be better, do better, and have a better life. *Better* referring to measurements of appearance, performance, and affluence, because that's where we are told the rewards lie. On the Dual Path, *better* refers to achieving a blend and balance of the sacred, of Heaven, in our lives.

For many, the paths of Heaven and Earth are separate. While we may taste the sacred and spiritual through our dreams, travels, religion, books, a near-death experience, an inner sense, or a practice such as yoga or meditation, we frequently struggle to integrate that sacredness into our lives. Those who are pulled towards the Heavenly Path often find themselves confused, unable to reconcile the direction it pulls them in and the changes it inspires them to make. Torn between the two, our life lacks a vital ingredient, unable to pursue the sacred within and discontent with a life devoted to work and obligations.

Then there are those who answer the call of the Heavenly Path: regular meditators, even masters of meditation; yoga instructors, or even gurus who, although dedicated, fail to recognize their own unhealthy patterns of thought and behavior.

It is only by actively being on the Dual Path that we can engage our spirits and souls as guides, recruiting our Earthly experiences as fuel to transport us to a cohesive life. The path of Sacred Practices is one of exploration, opening, understanding and the releasing of our Earthly patterns, while the path of Bodywork is one of *experiencing* our infinite potential (Heaven) within our physical and energetic matrix.

The Sacred Practices consist of the effort and dedication, the grunt work of change that *actively* invites conscious awareness into our world, clearing our densely forested lives and creating pathways to clarity.

Sacred Practices and Bodywork go hand in hand—without Sacred Practices, the value of Sacred Bodywork experiences are lost and are but vacations from the real world: we may be transported to magical realms, but we return to our lives as we were before. Furthermore, we would lack the practical application necessary to make actual progress: our habits and behaviors would never change and we would forever remain but occasional visitors to Heaven.

Although at times we may need to be more on one path than the other, the two paths intersect, double back, and cross over. Alone, each path is powerful, but when we walk them consciously *and* simultaneously, each magnifies the other, forging a Dual Path that gently inspires a deep and ongoing metamorphosis.

Walking the Dual Path is to create a meeting point within for Heaven and Earth to coexist, not in conflict but in sacred unification.

A Melding of Earth and Heaven

Earth

We are so connected to the Earth that our connection can easily go unnoticed and become completely neglected.

In every corner of the world we sift soil through our fingers, work in it, feed ourselves from it, and even though we may imprison it in concrete, we all, every one of us, stand on it.

It is on Earth that we are born, begin our journey and live our everyday lives.

Earth, having been here for so long (and we, in contrast being so transient), can appear rigid, inflexible, unmoving and unchanging. Many of us develop Earthly imbalances, rigid in our habits, personalities and needs. In its unbalanced manifestation we see before us only the things in life that need to be done; the endless lists, what we think of the *daily grind* of our lives. It is as if Earth itself has stopped spinning and ground to a halt, every day the same as the last.

Like the other forces of nature—fire, water and wind—Earth moves and changes considerably over its own track of time. Within it is the cycle of life, growth, transformation and death and a formidable gravitational force, a place of connection, to self and to nature.

Heaven

Just as we are all of the Earth, we are also of the Heavens that surround us. We think of Heaven as being up and out there, separate from us, and Heavens elusiveness can make it easy for us to ignore, disavow or miss altogether.

Traditionally, Heaven is the place that holds our hopes and dreams and the reward at the end of a *good life*. It is something that we work *towards*, not something that we *experience* on a day-to-day basis.

But Heaven *is* with us in our everyday life. It is in the moments that often go unnoticed, such as timelessness, spaciousness, intuition or total presence.

Heaven is (or can become) a state of being, calm, clear, steady, and weightless, free of fear, worry and anxiety. It is the spacious mind and body that is fluid, that lets go of holding patterns, that breathes deeply and softens, that is not attached to time or space. Heaven is where our life moves fluidly in its own current.

Any experience with Heaven is meaningful because it reminds or teaches us that we are not bound by Earth's parameters. During those moments in Heaven we experience dimensions and worlds beyond our physical body, thoughts, daily concerns and challenges, as we touch the undifferentiated potential within that is everywhere.

Melding

The melding of Heaven and Earth is at the center of all our creation stories. There have always been gods and miracles, and even in modern times when we refer to 'a miracle of science,' we refer to a melding of Heaven (miracle) and Earth (science).

In its extreme or purest form, Heaven is where the door opens and we lose our feet and our sense of balance as Earth drops away and we find ourselves lost in the ether. We may feel spacey, achieve nothing, and have no sense of direction.

In Earth's extreme or purist form, we are completely mired in our everyday tasks and obligations, just going from one to the next to the next. We may spend hours watching television or playing games; the couch potato is earth-bound. We are stuck, in a routine, with no movement forward, and we lack hope and inspiration.

When we bring Heaven down to meet our Earthly

> Rather than our lives moving towards death at every step, we move further into the richness of life and inner growth.

responsibilities we are not confined, defined and constricted by them. It gives us a means to create space and let go. When we bring Earth up to Heaven, we no longer float through life, grabbing for anything that anchors us to a structure. It is in these worlds meeting and shaping each other, the melding and balance, that we live our life to its fullest potential.

Since we do live here on Earth, most of us tend to be Earth-bound. We often live a life so driven to work, to be fit, to keep up, overdosing on ideas of duty and responsibility, that we drive ourselves through our life like cattle. However, if we meld Heaven and Earth, we shift our natures away from a harshness of being and create space, softness and a sense of sacredness that is sorely missing. It is in the melding that we are able to touch and be touched by life itself. Rather than our lives moving towards death at every step, we move further into the richness of life and inner growth.

The History and Future Change

Many of us, including myself, grew up with the old adage, *the more things change, the more they remain the same.* It had a lasting and profound effect on our willingness and perceived ability to change. But even if it was true when Jean-Baptiste Alphonse Karr wrote it back in the 1800's, it is not true in today's world. The tools for change have multiplied exponentially and we find ourselves surrounded and inundated by change.

When it comes to changing ourselves, many readily believe not only that we *cannot* ("Days change, seasons change, people don't change"—from the police drama *16 Blocks*) but also that we should not ("Don't go changing..." and, "I love you just the way you are!"—from Billy Joel's hit, *Just the Way You Are*). Reinforcing this idea are people whose features and attitudes seem to be chiseled in stone, and those who believe their impatience, anger, size, habits or a multitude of other characteristics are god-given and unalterable.

The truth is, there is *nothing* about ourselves that we *cannot* change. It is this truth that frightens us, because this truth means that that there are no excuses, it means we are conscious beings, making choices, including the bad ones, and that it rests on our shoulders to do the work.

ॐ

At one point in time, our culture was one of profundity, taking pride in doing one thing and doing it well. Our mode of learning was through apprenticeship, dedicating our lives to honing a skill. There were master woodworkers, sword makers, philosophers, orators and so on. Now we are a culture that takes pride in multi-tasking, and our attention spans have grown short. We've become accustomed to quick-fix, quick-bake, microwaveable lives, taking a pill rather than doing the work, fixing or preventing a problem.

This has led to a loss of faith and confidence in ourselves, and a tendency to give up prematurely—even in learning a new skill such as yoga, language classes, or golf —

convinced we can only do so much and that we cannot actually accomplish the level of competency we see in those who are more skilled or more advanced. In fact, there are so few really skilled people around that we have trouble discerning the skilled from the unskilled. We may not stop the process of learning altogether, but somewhere inside we withdraw from our initial dreams and aspirations and instead make-do with a modified version. When we *make-do* with this simplified version of ourselves, we in effect, dumb ourselves down and give up on our dreams and our potential. This is a very serious choice to make and we do not fully understand the extent of the toll it takes on us. In making this choice, we literally kill off a piece of our spirit, the spark that gives us life, until we find that our life has lost its vibrancy, its meaning and its sense of purpose.

We all live and we all die, and we all spend the time between those dates right here on this Earth. The *choice* we have is how we spend that time. Are you the pilot who floats through the clouds and sails on the winds, enthralled by the sights, sounds and sensations or the one whose eyes are clenched tight, afraid to look down and around? Fears, like everything else, can be overcome. Rather than ignoring the signs and waiting for the mid-life crisis, the illness, the marriage to end, the kids to go off to college or you to retire, the time in your life when you feel completely lost, you can be proactive and reconnect to your true and intrinsic nature.

It *can* be done; we *can* change, no matter what we've done in our past, who we've been, what we believe of ourselves, or even what others believe about us. Change and growth is a matter of the choices we make, hard work, perseverance, willingness and dedication, which is exactly what this path is about. The going is tough, but once the path is somewhat worn, it becomes smoother, until the day comes when you wake up and look behind at who you used to be. Tough going to *an* end, or tough going to *the* end... it's your choice.

Deepening Our Contact with Life

The elusive hold of touch upon our being begins pre-birth with the rhythmic caresses of amniotic fluid. The magnetic force of touch is so strong that in prenatal massage, babies in utero often move their little bodies towards my hands as I make contact with their mother's belly.

Touch is our life's breath. It is through touch that our breath comes to life, the hands that pull us free, the hands that gently slap our bottom, and then arms that hold and cradle us. We are literally cradled by touch from the moment of conception. Whatever happens from here on we all, *every one of us*, with few exceptions, begin and experience life in this same way.

Whenever and wherever we look, we see hands in constant motion and contact: cradling phones, keyboards, newspapers, steering wheels, cups of coffee and bags, while hand-holding hand is relegated, for the most part, between parents and children or as indicators of new love. This constant swirling of touch, like a beautiful buffet that we cannot actually eat, acts as a reminder of our fear of lingering; a fear of opening the heart and touching the soul of the self or the other, and how, although we long for a deep and soulful relationship, we ourselves may not be ready to touch or be touched deeply.

Many of us unwittingly search for a sense of fulfillment in companionship, food and drink, in love or in sex, and as our search becomes all-consuming, we become increasingly desperate. Our desperation leads us to *fashion* ourselves into something 'desirable' and we look to the *role models* of desirability in our society: those distorted images of beauty and desire that we see on billboards, at bus stops, in magazines and on television. While many just dream of being like them (which is no less harmful), others make overt changes to their clothing, perfume, aftershave, hair and makeup, and others actually reshape themselves, cutting, pulling, stretching and re-sowing their skin, in an effort to create newer and better versions of themselves in attempt to look like their heroes, defy gravity and pretend that aging is not part of life. All this, in our search for that which has been lost, that which our hearts truly cry out for.

We are so busy fashioning ourselves into someone who can be loved, we forget that folded deeply and safely inside, there is a sacred being. We know, we *feel* that some deep part of us has been neglected and goes unseen, but profoundness cannot be faked. We cannot pretend and remain unbroken. Those who settle for 'something' rather than 'nothing' find their lives dwindling away as they become tired, old and brittle.

This path calls for healing those aspects of ourselves that have been hurt and broken, an opening of the heart, a stepping up of self-expectation, and an expansion and maturity of the spirit creating a new path ahead. As you begin the Sacred Practices, know that pre-judging and skipping the ones that don't 'speak to you' will obviously not give you the benefits of being fully committed and *doing them*. Albert Einstein said that the definition of insanity is "doing the same thing over and over again and expecting different results."

Let us go forward, as Stanley Keleman says, rather than with the shrinking of life's space, with a graceful beauty, an ever richening maturity and a deepening contact with life.

There can be a kind of aging which we could call a rich maturity.

A mature tree is gnarled, strong, and beautifully graceful. There is a quality of experience written into it that you can see.

It is not withered and dried up; the life is not gone.

Maturing is a deepening contact with life, and the ability to sustain and refine that contact. It does not have to be the shrinking life space that is usually described as old age and is the result of our own self-corseting.

STANLEY KELEMAN,
THE HUMAN GROUND

Part 2
The Sacred Practices

Putting on Our Galoshes

Taking the path of Sacred Practices is to choose to consciously and arduously chart the swampland rather than reside *in* it (or have it reside within *us*). As we put on our galoshes, we come to understand that what we have become, what we *are*, is a roadmap to the meaning and soul that lie *within* us. As our map unfolds, like knights on a quest, we honor the mountains we have to scale, the deserts and oceans we need to cross, the demons we must face and the dragons we need to slay, because without doing so we cannot nobly save, retrieve and re-birth the child within. This path is a journey of a lifetime, and of a life that is ever transforming with endless possibilities.

The Precipice

The Sacred Practices bid us to *willingly* allow ourselves to make both subtle and radical shifts in our habits, speech, friends, belongings, tendencies and in our very nature. One aspect of this path is to go forth on our adventures, exploring what has contributed to that which we find within. Another aspect is to empty our luggage, and begin anew.

We're going to walk in to this swampland,

and the purpose is not to walk in and construct a home and live there, it is to put on some galoshes,

and walk through and find our way around.

BRENÉ BROWN,
LISTENING TO SHAME

This is not a quick-fix plan, nor is it a trivial or easy task. It is typical to feel that this is *hard* work; that it is really difficult to face the things about yourself you don't like, and to find that you're afraid to disconnect from favored but detrimental behaviors. What if being controlling, pouting, angry, or sexualizing yourself gets you what you want?

You *will* have to ask yourself hard questions. You will have to go to the mirror and look for truth. You *will* find yourself at the precipice and not know where it leads. One of the characters in the 2008 movie, *The Day the Earth Stood Still* says, "It's only on the brink that people find the will to change. Only at the precipice do we evolve." In the end it is not the precipice that holds our attention, not the *hard work* involved in getting there, but the magic of who we have evolved into.

Rooted in Earth

Through the Sacred Practices we develop inner stability, strength and connection. Without powerful roots such as these, similarly to a plant, we cannot be healthy and will most likely grow crooked, becoming weak, lost and confused in purpose or direction. This is a universal dilemma.

We've all seen or know of people who are gnarled in body or twisted in spirit, but when we look at a baby, we never expect them to grow into that person. Often without our consent, our babies, children, pre-teens and teenagers find themselves in a cold and lonely world, where at every stage they are required to give up their dreams so they can just survive. It is never too early or too late to be on this path—these practices create a fundamental foundation that can be used as a directing force, or a force of re-direction.

We have learned to measure our health and success with a lack of disease and an abundance of money. The Sacred Practices take us along a path not with a philosophy but with a way of being where dreams are honored and success is measured by the health and vibrancy of the organism.

Jack's beanstalk was strong and healthy, allowing him to climb his way to the heavens. The roots' main function, rather than to root us, is to create a base of strength and health so that we grow towards and connect to Heaven.

There are three Foundation Practices and eighteen Sacred Practices and together they lay out a map to accompany, guide, support and nurture us on our path of exploration and discovery, enabling us to live to the fullest in beauty and sacredness as we become one with this organism we call life.

Many of these practices will become part of who you are; how you think and see things. While some will stay with you and have a prevailing and continued influence, others will periodically call you back when you need them.

May your strong,
healthy roots

keep your hands in
the fire of the soul

and may your wings

transport you to
the Heavens

Three Foundation Practices

Dual Path Meditation begins like most mediation practices as a solitary practice. The subsequent phases slowly integrates meditation into your everyday life until it becomes an effortless part of who you are and how you function.

EFT (Emotional Freedom Technique) sessions use a tapping technique on the body's meridians to clear energy that is stored in our system. This effective technique is very easy to learn. I recommend learning the system so you can use it whenever you have a moment and the need arises as well as working with an EFT professional (which is quite different than doing EFT on yourself) once a week, or as often as possible, while going through the Sacred Practices.

Sacred Bodywork sessions are recommended once a week, if possible, while you are going through the Sacred Practices. Optimally, your sessions will be with a professional who is trained in this bodywork, but ultimately the sessions can be with any bodywork professional whose work transports you to a different realm. Reading Parts 3 and 4 will inform you of what is possible and how to harness the power of your Sacred Bodywork experiences.

Eighteen Sacred Practices

Decide how often you will do a practice: once a day, every other day or once a week. Since the program is set up to create transformation, do not spread them out too much: optimally, no less than one a week. However, if there is a time lapse, just return to them.

The Sacred Practices balance our *working out* with *working in*. The reasons for working out are apparent to us—it relieves stress relief, improves cardiovascular function, increases muscle tone, and of course it helps us look and feel good. The benefits are apparent and often visible and noticeable, so we do it.

However, we tend to see *mental* health as independent of *physical* health and something we either have or do not have, failing to recognize that we are an organism, that everything is interrelated. Often, clients come in with an arm in a sling and don't understand why their neck or back hurts or why they are more depressed.

It is through the Sacred Practices that our practical understanding of health expands, interconnecting our physical and emotional body, our mental processes, pace of life, our habits and our life choices.

These practices are not designed to change others, but to change your relationship with yourself, to change your fundamental core being

What You Will Need

To set some time aside. Some of the Practices may take an hour while others may take a good part of a day. Give yourself enough time so that you have plenty of time to contemplate and don't have to cut your practice short.

A journal and pen.

Shifting Terrain

Most of us start life with a healthy and intact energetic matrix. As we go through life, difficult experiences cause shifts and disruptions that can then harden into patterns of behavior, or physical holding. These experiences may be large, such as being assaulted, or may even go relatively unnoticed such as being told what to expect in life, who we *should* be, how we *should* act, or being yelled at by a teacher, sibling or parent. Whether they are large or small, stand out as a traumatic experience or get lost in the myriad of life's interactions, they all shift the terrain. Over time the health of our energetic matrix may devolve until we find ourselves disconnected from our true nature, even forgetting that we once had a true nature.

Using these practices to judge yourself to be a 'good person' or a 'bad person,' or to learn what is *right* or *wrong* and to adhere to some code of conduct is not the way to approach this. Think of it as simply mapping the terrain of who you are. As you go through these Practices, the terrain will naturally and gently shift back into its healthy configuration.

We're used to thinking of terrains and environments as things that exist *independently and external* to ourselves, but they are neither independent nor external. Our terrain and environment is comprised of our surroundings, the pharmacy within our body, our fluids and tissue, our thought patterns, behaviors, emotions: all the components of our energetic matrix. These aspects do not and cannot exist independently from us, each other, the choices we make or the life we live and create for ourselves.

Allowing the terrain to shift and being with the challenges that follow requires willingness, openness and readiness. You are the guide, the warrior and the hero who has brought you to this moment. Allow yourself to continue down this Dual Path with wisdom, courage and integrity.

Health
is a balance of
activity and inactivity.

Sounds and silence.

Action and
contemplation.

Movement and
stillness.

Effort and ease.

Health is a
balance of working out
and working in:
Earth and Heaven

Three Foundation Practices

 *Foundation Practice 1*

Dual Path Meditation

Dual Path Meditation mirrors our journey along the Dual Path as it begins with an internal focus and brings us to absolute connection.

This meditation practice plays a supporting role for all the practices that follow. It has one foot in Earth and one in Heaven, and is a pathway that joins the two. The foot in Earth (the internal focus), deals with the mud that keeps us stuck in our past and our habits, and the foot in Heaven allows these to drop away as we glimpse at the vast universe beyond ourselves (absolute connection).

This is the most precious of practices, one that becomes a daily visitor we welcome warmly, a friend we eagerly embrace as we sit and share insights, visions and journeys. It is not always the quiet, calm and contemplative experience we have been told to expect of meditation; we take our seat on our friend, the dragon, open the window and let go of the reins. For some, this is the most challenging practice of all.

Open the Window to Ride the Dragon

When we meditate, we literally open the window to our mind and our soul, where the dragon within has been bridled, caged, and muffled. When we first agree to sit, the dragon has a lot to say. It yells and shouts; its caged energy apparent in its irritation. This simple act of sitting invites the dragon and a whole host of uninvited guests. We can do nothing but *watch* as they parade themselves in front of us in the guise of useless and mundane thoughts, feelings, worries, plans and habits (internal focus). All we can do is hang on for the ride and watch the scenery go by until the moment or the day comes when the dragon is worn out, has said its piece and can then be at peace. Each day the dragon will be there, waiting to play its games, waiting to take out the mirror so you can see your inner self.

Dragons are the constant, shifting, uninvited, intrusive guests who take any and every opportunity to be with us, *not only* when we are meditating. When we think about taking a bath or sitting down to have a cup of tea or to meditate, they will tell us we don't have time. When we are on vacation they will constantly nag at us, reminding us of how much work we will have to do when we get home again. When we are getting a massage they will remind us that we still need to shop for dinner, or how much our right foot itches, and when we are giving a massage they will bring us daydreams and distractions. Dual Path Meditation is a practice that allows us to be present to each moment, wherever we are and whatever the circumstances. Life is full of opportunity for the dragon to visit, and for us to return to silence. Notice the dragon when it tries to pull you onto its back. Silence is a place within you that you must find, nurture and tread a well-worn path to.

If you enter into the practice of meditation expecting the calm and quiet mind to present itself, you will probably come to feel you have a dirty secret: *your* mind cannot be quieted; *your* mind is erratic and crazy. If you don't understand why you would want to open the window in the first place, you will mistake meditation as something that is a painful, boring, and pointless waste of time.

The truth is that the dragon is the path to wisdom and clarity, and those of us who embrace it as a friend do so because we need the light it sheds in seeking to expose ourselves to the full light of day. We open the window because we are tired of living in the dark. We open the window because even though it is difficult to ride the dragon, this is undoubtedly our dragon revealing our naked truth, like a secret diary, to our eyes only.

What an amazing opportunity! Every day we open the window as an invitation to the light, allowing it to shine, as if on a diamond—on our disparate facets—as it reflects back to us moment-to-moment and day-to-day.

Beyond these moments, we may suddenly notice the dragon is no longer with us. Instead, we have our own wings, and are soaring and diving, spirit and soul together into the vast unending field. We will never see and never even know this field exists if we do not first choose to ride the dragon and come face-to-face with our own reflection.

There are four stages to Dual Path Meditation. Begin with the first stage, moving through to the others when you feel ready to do so. One stage does not take the place of another: at some point you will be doing all four stages of this Dual Path Meditation. Whether you are new to meditation or not, take some time with this practice. When you sit with the dragons, it is important to remember this is our life, not a race; be gentle and true to yourself.

Stage 1: Sitting Practice

This Sitting Practice often naturally becomes a ritual as we create a comfortable space to sit in and return to again and again. Optimally, the Sitting Practice is a 20-minute daily practice, or even twice-daily practice with eyes closed.

Find or create a comfortable place to sit—a chair, couch, zafu and zabuton, or your bed—and a comfortable position (cross legged, feet on the ground or legs extended) and if you find you are not comfortable, just switch positions. This practice is not about sitting still for as long as possible, so if you find yourself in discomfort during your meditation, adjust your position. At some point down the path, you will naturally find yourself slipping into stillness.

As you take your position, consciously acknowledge to yourself that you are taking your seat to enter into meditation, not to daydream, to plan an event, or to solve a problem, or to take a trip down memory lane. To acknowledge this shift in mindset, it can be helpful to mark this time by striking a bell or lighting a candle or some incense.

As you begin, invite yourself to enter into silence. Silence may come to you easily or you may have immediate difficulty and realize that you have company. The dragons work in mysterious ways and before you know it you may realize you are not alone, and that the Irritated Dragon, the Memory Lane Dragon, the Mind Wandering Dragon, the Itchy Legged Dragon or any number of other Dragons have pulled you onto their backs.

At first you may be attached to your dragon, unable to separate yourself. We often move through our life with visiting dragons flying in and out of our days, undetected and yet having a profound effect on every aspect of our life. *Noticing their presence* is the first step, and once their presence has been noted we can then decide on whether we invite them to linger.

Begin by inviting them in, sitting down and relaxing together. Hear what they have to say as if they bring you wisdom. And when you are ready, perhaps tired of your visitor, again invite silence back in, open the door and ask them to leave. Do not leave it up to them to leave on their own. This is an important distinction. *You* must be the one who opens the door and pushes them over the threshold. Rather than a push, it is more of a gentle and subtle nudge. Do not end your meditation here. It is important to notice the silence that follows, to see if they try to return or if another dragon slips in trying to fill the space that has been vacated.

As you become better and more comfortable with getting your dragons to leave, begin to shorten the time between noticing their arrival and opening the door. You have invited silence in, so don't spend a lot of time with dragons that come to visit. Notice them and open the door. Practice gives rise to a well-worn pathway toward clearing our mind, letting go of our beliefs, patterns of thought and emotions. Eventually, it leads to the space and silence that exists between and without these dragons.

Stage 2: Returning

Returning is a principle that most meditations work with. It is particularly useful if you struggle with getting your dragons to leave, if they insist on coming back again, or if you are so used to living in the company of your dragons that you believe this is your normal state.

You have been working with returning to internal silence, but now choose something else to return to, such as a word, candle flame, your third eye, the sound of running water (such as a fountain, river), smoke from burning incense or your breath. As you find yourself in the company of a dragon, gently return to the object of focus.

Stage 3: Go Public

It is not enough to restrict this meditation to a cushion; now transition your practice to public places, while commuting or sitting in a coffee shop or park. Notice how the sight of something or someone will elicit a thought or even a reaction. Encourage its departure by inviting it to leave. Like a train entering the station and departing again, notice the arrival of a thought and its departure.

If you are working with Returning in public spaces, it will be less problematic to Return to silence, breath, your third eye, a word or mantra, then to a candle flame or the other options.

Stage 4: Put Your Practice to Work

Integrate meditation everywhere you can, in your work and relationships, and you will begin to see deep changes in yourself, your degree of calm, focus and grounding, and how others interact with you.

Meditation Tips
Downloading is Part of the Process

Aristotle said *"Nature abhors a vacuum,"* which explains why when we sit down to meditate, we're often inundated with thoughts rather than the tranquility we are after. The act of sitting alone in a quiet environment creates space, or a vacuum, and our thoughts rush in to fill that space. This is where many people judge themselves and what they perceive as their "failed" attempt at meditation and quit. This stage, I call "downloading," is integral to the process. Without taking the time to download, we function within the chaos of our Mental Body and Emotional Body.

In Transcendental Meditation this process has been explained as a bottle of soda with bubbles rising to the surface—our thoughts are these bubbles rising to the surface, just energy. We don't need to hold on or stay attached to them. Allow the bubbles to rise, don't fight or try to suppress them. Soda bubbles easily rise and then vanish all on their own.

Practice Gently

Watch your thought as it departs, looking at it as you would a cloud floating, or a bird flying by. As you do this, realize that just as the cloud and the bird are not a part of you, neither are your thoughts: they just come into your field of vision and awareness and leave again. They neither belong to you nor can you possess them. It is just energy that comes to you and stays for as long as it is welcome. The nature of thought is that you will have repeated opportunities to let them go. As thoughts come, *gently* let them go.

Practice with Your Breath

If you have trouble releasing your thoughts try using your exhalation as a transportation system, literally releasing your thoughts to the air or wind in any of the following ways:

- Be aware of both your in and out breaths and release the thought as you exhale
- Actively blow the thought out
- Imagine your thought dissolving, as you exhale
- See your thought as a density of energy that is released as it dissipates in the particles of your breath

Common Thought Themes

- I really have to get going with my day.
- That's it? I just sit here and 'notice'? I don't get it! I'm just wasting my time! I don't have time for this! Why am I doing this?
- I'm uncomfortable, maybe I'll just shift my position a little
- Why am I tense?
- What should I do with my breath?
- I could try this in the other room (or on the other chair).
- I'm cold; I need a blanket, socks...

There are emotions, family patterns, and there are also genes. What is the space in between them?

EINSTEIN SAID:

"The spaces between events are greater than the events themselves."

BERTRAND RUSSELL SAID:

"It's the space between the notes that makes the music."

MARTIN BUBER:

"We have to be at the center of the I and the We."

BUDDHISM:

"Take the middle path"

LAO-TZU SAID OF TAOISM:

"There is no this, there is no that. There is the still point where this and that exists."

And that's where life happens, in the still point.

DR. PAUL H. BRENNER, EPIGENETICS AND THE SPACE AROUND US, TED.COM

- I really have to remember to pick up some strawberry jam, more kale, the dry cleaning, try that new recipe... (fill in the blank)
- I'm tired, maybe I should just take a nap.
- It really made me mad when.... (go over conversations you've had)

Just notice, and Return staying connected to the discovery of your journey. It will lead you to an absolutely unique, more sacred you.

Practice Meditation

Practice every day. This is a *practice*. Embrace your dragon as it whispers or yells at you, repeatedly reflecting your craziness, confident that as the process itself filters and refines your energy, it leads you to sanity, clarity and peace.

Practice this exercise daily or every other day, working up from however long you *can* sit, to as long as you *want* to sit. If you shift into another state of being, quietness, spaciousness, wandering away from your physical body, notice that too but don't try to hold on to it or recreate it when you sit the next time.

 *Foundation Practice 2*

Emotional Freedom Technique (EFT)

EFT works with the meridian system of the body, the channels of energy that like train tracks, have specific routes, each with its own starting and ending points. There are 12 major channels in the body, each associated with an internal organ, and 8 extraordinary meridians, each one a reservoir of energy. Acupuncture works with these meridians primarily by inserting needles to stimulate the flow of energy (qi or chi) and correct imbalances. Acupressure has the same goals, but rather than using needles, applies pressure along these lines. EFT works with these meridians by simply tapping on particular areas of the body where a number of these meridians come together or are close to the surface.

While tapping, you will focus on a specific issue, thought, feeling or event to clear its energy from your system. EFT has been found to be remarkably beneficial in making shifts in the emotional, psychological and/or physical body.

Either hand can do the tapping—most people naturally tap with their dominant hand, but you can use either. Some people even use both hands at the same time. The only point where this cannot be done is the first one, the karate chop point.

There are two parts to the EFT sequence, the Set Up Phrase and the Reminder Phrase. The following is the basic sequence:

Set Up Phrase
The Karate Chop Point (Small Intestine Meridian)

The first point is known as the 'karate chop' point and is located on the fleshy part of the side of the hand. Tapping is done with the fingers lightly but firmly. As you tap this point, say the set-up phrase, which begins:

Even though… and then choose any statement that is true for you. The following are just examples, but choose any difficulty you encounter you as you work with the practices:

- *I'm too busy and can't make time for this…*
- *I don't want to repeat the patterns I have repeated over and over again*
- *I don't have anyone's support*
- *No one understands me*
- *I know I just have to do this*
- *My life has been so hard*
- *I want to have a better life*
- *I know I'm so angry*
- *I have worked so hard*
- *I'm so anxious about everything*
- *I feel (un)worthy of something better*
- *I don't have the strength/courage/willpower*

Finish the sentence with one of the following statements. The stronger the affirmation, the better:

- *I completely and deeply love and respect myself*
- *I love myself*
- *I'm okay*
- *I've survived*
- *I'm okay with that*
- *This is how it is right now*
- *I'm still a good person*
- *I completely accept how I feel*
- *I'm open to accepting myself just the way I am*

An example of the complete set up phrase would be: *Even though I don't know where my life is going, I completely and deeply love and accept myself.* Say your set up statement 3 times, tapping on the karate chop point the whole time.

Reminder Phrase

Tap each of the following meridian points repeating a reminder phrase taken directly from your set-up statement to keep you focused on your issue. If your set-up phrase was, *Even though I'm anxious about starting on this path because I don't know where it's going to go, I completely and deeply love and accept myself*, you're reminder phrase might be one or a combination of the following (choose the words that are real and true for you, and use your tone of voice to place emphasize):

- *I'm anxious*
- *I don't know what's going to happen*
- *I'm so anxious*
- *I wish I wasn't so anxious*

For all the following tapping points:

1. Top of the Head (Hundred Meeting Points Meridian)

Be particularly gentle with this tapping point.

2. Above the Eyebrow (Bladder Meridian)

Located to the side of the bridge of the nose where the eyebrow begins.

3. Side of the Eye (Gall Bladder Meridian)

Located at the end of the eyebrow.

4. Under the Eye (Stomach Meridian)

5. Under the Nose (Governing Meridian)

6. The Chin (Central Meridian)

This point is actually on the fleshy part under the lip rather than on the bony part of the chin.

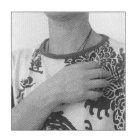

7. Collar Bone (Kidney Meridian)

This point is called Kidney 27. Although it is called the Collar bone point, it is not directly on the collar bone but underneath it. This point is said to balance adrenal function.

 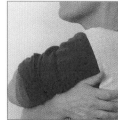

8. Under the Arm (Spleen Meridian)

Reach around to the side of your body and tap beneath the armpit on the ribs.

Go through points 1 through 8, starting at the top of the head a total of three times, repeating the reminder phrase.

Now check in with yourself and see if the issue or thought you've been working with feels less intense. Rate it from 10 (really high) to zero and repeat the whole sequence including the set-up phrase to bring it down further.

This will serve to support you as you work with the practices in addition to your work with an EFT professional. To find an EFT professional in your area, do an Internet search or go to www.aamet.org for a worldwide listing.

Once you have begun the Sacred Practices, try to do at least one session a week with a professional. In between you can do EFT on yourself. If you already know how to do EFT on yourself, it is still important to do EFT with a professional while you do the Practices. A professional can see and hear things that you may not be aware of and take the session in a direction you wouldn't otherwise go.

In Europe, EFT is an accepted modality, and in America, EFT is quickly growing in popularity. Even though many people have not heard of it, at the time of writing this, Nick Ortner has a book called *The Tapping Solution* on the New York Times Bestseller list. For most people, the *idea* of EFT seems hokey, and that feeling stays with them even when they begin to do it. Fortunately, you don't have to understand it or believe in it for it to actually work; you just have to give it a try.

Foundation Practice 3

Sacred Bodywork

Bodywork is one of those rare deeds that one must do in person and it is this unique agreement, that one human will lay their hands on another, that yields the power to shift and transcend disruptions in the energetic matrix.

Since it is not possible to get a session, or any bodywork session, by reading this book or going on the Internet, Part 4, *Finding a Sacred Bodyworker*, offers guidance on how to find and choose a Professional to work with, keeping in mind that the goal of these sessions is larger than *feeling better, being in less discomfort* and *feeling more relaxed*. You want to look for an experience that takes you from the world you came in with (Earth) to another (Heaven), even if just for a moment. So even if you have a massage professional you are otherwise completely satisfied with, this may not be their area of mastery or even a concept they are familiar with.

As you read on you'll see that Sacred Bodywork has a specific focus: to detect areas of energetic density and to diffuse them.

If your particular life situation allows, get at least one Sacred Bodywork session a week while you work with the Practices. Otherwise, get them as often as your situation allows for.

THE GUEST HOUSE

This being human is a guesthouse.
Every morning a new arrival.

A joy, a depression, a meanness,
some momentary awareness comes
as an unexpected visitor.

Welcome and entertain them all!
Even if they are a crowd of sorrows,
who violently sweep your house
empty of its furniture,
still, treat each guest honorably.
He may be clearing you out
for some new delight.

The dark thought, the shame, the
malice, meet them at the door
laughing, and invite them in.

Be grateful for whoever comes
because each has been sent
as a guide from beyond.

FROM *THE ESSENTIAL RUMI,*
TRANSLATIONS BY COLEMAN BARKS

Be sure to read The Client and Professional Guide, particularly Getting the Most Out of Your Session.

The Powerful Duo of Practices & Bodywork

While for the client or layperson the combination of Sacred Bodywork and Sacred Practices serve to magnify and fortify each, for the professional it creates a particular sensibility: a field within, and for their client, that is sacred.

For Massage Professionals

Part 3 of this book, Sacred Bodywork, explains and describes the concepts and techniques of Sacred Bodywork.

Eighteen Sacred Practices

 *Practice Session 1*

Awakening the Spirit Song

This ritual is an adaptation of the Cherokee Song of the Sacred Pipe, passed on to me by Hugh Milne. Ritual has a transformative power, and through repetition and familiarity the power in this particular ritual changes and grows over time. Awakening the Spirit Song invites the energies from the four directions. View the video at adualpath.com/spiritsong for the stepping and movement pattern.

Do this ritual several times a week so it becomes a source of grounding, focus and strength. Notice your voice and how it changes as an indicator of where you are within yourself. Try it in different places, indoors and outside, noticing what feels different and what feels best. Also notice as you become more familiar with it and say it from memory rather reading it off a page, how its power deepens.

There are two parts to the song: the Opening and Closing.

We begin by facing East with both hands on the heart. As you open to the spirit of the next directions, you will turn to face each one, each time beginning with hands on the heart as you invite the energy in. The

Opening is repeated three times. Each time is slightly different.

1. Say the complete opening out loud to the four directions.
2. Repeat the sequence, this time only the final three words of each of the directions are said out loud (for East you would say out loud, "clarity and perception").
3. Repeat a third time, now saying the last three words in silence.

Opening

I open to the East, the place of the Visionary, of clarity and perception.
I ask this fine morning to be filled with clarity and perception.

I open to the South, the place of the Healer, of energy and innocence.
I ask this fine morning to be filled with energy and innocence.

I open to the West, the place of the Teacher, of wisdom and understanding.
I ask this fine morning to be filled with wisdom and understanding.

I open to the North, the place of the Warrior, of courage and perseverance
I ask this fine morning to be filled with courage and strength.

Closing

You now turn to face East again and remain facing this direction for the Closing.

May the Holy Wind fill my Heart with the song of rainbows, and connect me to all things.
May the Great Earth nurture me with her raw, red energy and fill my veins with vitality.
May this path guide me to grow and evolve.
May it Awaken my Spirit, help me dissolve.
I honor and bow to the Sacred within.

Soften Your Gaze

This simple and effective practice re-establishes the connection between our eyes and our hearts, transforming our internal energy. It is through our eyes that we meet the world, encouraging or dissuading connection, showing affection or love, setting boundaries or expressing displeasure. This energy filtering through our eyes connects directly to our hearts. By simply softening our gaze, we soften and open our hearts and allow any negativity within to naturally dissipate.

If the heart is closed and hardened, we may jeopardize our health and the relationships we value as we create an environment of negativity around and within us. Signs of this may be in feeling that people don't want to spend time with us, that life is tedious and lacks joy, a disconnection to self and others, or as if we are carrying a suitcase on our backs that is so heavy that we cannot move. This path is one of unburdening, one that ferries us to a lightness of being and a warmness of heart.

As we pass people walking down the street, our eyes wash over them. We step into a store or café and someone sees us and glances up. We get in line and notice the counter staff or the person in line ahead of us. We see a friend and a smile comes to our eyes, we soften and relax.

Phase 1

Smile with your eyes. If the smile expresses itself in other ways, do not suppress it; it is just a sign that your heart and your whole system needs to feel warmth and connection. In fact, it is not unusual to go through a period of not being able to separate smiling with your eyes and a full facial smile. This is beneficial as it will begin to fill the reservoir of your heart with positive energy. As your heart fills and the pathway of energy between the eyes and the heart strengthens, it will be easier to shift from an external *appearance* of smiling to a purely internal experience. Once this shift occurs, this very subtle practice will soften your inner world and transform your internal energy. Always return to the eyes: It is through the eyes that the energy travels to the heart.

When

Do this practice first thing in the morning, smiling to yourself and those around you, when you walk into a café, supermarket, at work, when you greet someone, whenever and wherever you see yourself and others. As you do this, you will become more aware of, and sensitive to the energy that people greet you with and hold within themselves. Be careful not to hold or mirror their energy.

Now include inanimate objects as well as people, and you will soon find it occurs naturally and without effort, no longer in response to an external trigger. A feeling of increased warmth and openness is a sign of internal transformation.

 *Practice Session 3*

Windows to the Soul: Our Sacred Mirrors

Eyes (Earth), Soul (Heaven), Window: the Pathway Between the Two

The Windows to the Soul practice clears the path between Heaven and Earth that otherwise would hinder movement from one world to the other.

Our eyes are our Sacred Mirrors, they are not only a vehicle by which we see and take in information, but a place we hold and reflect our thought and emotional patterns and how we communicate with others and ourselves. Visualize a line, a pathway made of words going from your eyes to whatever or whoever you are looking at. This path is a two-way path: whatever goes out also returns to you. If this pathway is made of negativity, how we see the world and ourselves is obstructed and becomes a dangerous pathway. Windows to the Soul begins by exploring what your path is made up of and begins the process of cleaning and clearing your Sacred Mirrors.

Phase 1

Stand or sit in front of a mirror and look into your own eyes. Make notes in your journal of:

- Your initial reaction
- What you see and feel
- What you say to yourself
- If your gaze wanders to your face, your hair, your neck, how does that shape your thoughts?
- The balance of positive and negative self-talk. Are you self-critical or self-deprecating or even abusive? Identify the friend and the foe within.

Phase 2

This phase attunes you to your deeper nature and wisdom.

Ask your eyes the following and write the response in your journal:
- What have they been witness to in your lifetime?
- If your eyes could speak, what would they say? What do they want you to know?
- If they had advice for you, what would it be?

Phase 3

From now on, whenever you look at yourself, practice Soften Your Gaze until you greet yourself with warmth and see the wisdom and kindness within.

 *Practice Session 4*

Harness the Power of Nature

Even if we resist the urge to spend time in nature, we are magnetically pulled towards it, gazing at clouds, trees moving in the wind, a bird, the sunset and the ocean or whatever else is available. 'Nature' may be your garden, your local park, your favorite swimming hole, or the air, sun or rain on your morning run. We may not be aware that we are in the presence of power, but as we stand in the forces of nature it soaks in to our very bones and cells.

Spending quiet time with the natural, powerful rhythms of nature takes us away from the noise and preoccupations of our everyday life and reconnects us with our own forces, helping us to move beyond individual limitations. Similar to a massage, we often enter busy and preoccupied and by the end we feel calm, grounded, renewed and replenished. Harnessing the Power of Nature turns this natural process into the active ritual we crave when we look up at the clouds, nurturing a mind that needs quiet, contemplation and spaciousness.

Phase 1

Go into nature. Walk quietly by yourself until you find a place that calls to you to sit, stand or lie down. Settle in, be quiet and still.

Try not to be 'alert', just notice what you notice, perhaps ants walking on leaves and twigs, the movement of grass, weeds, trees and branches. Notice movement close to you and those further away. Notice sounds; the rustle of leaves, birds chirping or singing, the sound of the wind in the trees.

Phase 2

Close your eyes and forget that you are a person in nature.

Once we're in nature, we often naturally close our eyes and take a deep breath. This instinctual piece of the ritual allows the barriers between us and nature to dissolve, and for the two eco-systems to meld.

Around and within, external and internal, is an environment of sound, movement and stillness—a melody we are all part of. Allow yourself—your body, your being—to dissolve into your surroundings. Give yourself the time to just be, with no agenda, no purpose but to allow your surroundings to enter you, and you to enter your surroundings.

Phase 3

Honor the power you have harnessed.

Do not underestimate feelings of calm, focus, strength, grounding, connection, relaxation or any other change: this is the very power you have harnessed.

Resources: Read — or better yet, listen to *Beauty*, by John O'Donohue

 *Practice Session 5*

Mapping Your Internal Environment

Recognizing signs of energetic disruption and disquiet allows us to have a hand in shaping our lives by making informed choices.

Our hobbies, behaviors and actions are indications of how we feel about our life, and how we cope with it. When we are not living the life we want to live, not achieving our potential, we often artificially create a high, ride an emotional roller coaster, and live in a constant state of chaos or drama. This lifestyle becomes the norm; most people are under the impression that these habits are no more than characteristics of who they are, embracing them as that which gives them their individuality.

Phase 1

Look for the signposts that indicate disquiet in your internal environment. It can be difficult to accurately self-reflect, so take into consideration not only what *you* see in yourself, but how others see you. Check all that apply:

You Feel

○ Your life is crazy

○ The people around you drive you crazy

○ Unsettled

○ Bored or under-stimulated

○ You're not really doing what you want to be doing

○ You never have time for yourself

○ Sorry for what you've done or said

○ You're wasting your time

○ Life is meaningless

○ You do things that you know you shouldn't be doing or are bad for you

○ You apologize a lot, or are resistant to apologizing

Emotional States

○ You are moody

○ You are impatient

○ You need space or downtime

○ You are emotionally inconsistent

○ You can't settle into what you are doing

○ You get irritated, frustrated or angry

○ You find it difficult to control yourself

○ You cause physical or emotional pain with your words or actions

Physical States

○ You sense that you hold your breath or feel you are not breathing

○ You constantly have physical tension

○ You're unhappy with how you look

○ You avoid looking at yourself first thing in the morning

○ You're always checking how you look in a mirror or reflections in store windows

○ You're uncomfortable with yourself if your hair isn't done just right or you have no make-up on

○ You feel trapped in your body

○ You can't sit still, fidget

Driving Habits

○ You drive like a 'bat out of hell' and have a lot of 'close calls'

○ You drive faster than you need to and then stop abruptly at the stop sign or the traffic in front of you

○ You try to beat others when the traffic light changes

○ You habitually speed

○ Slow traffic irritates or aggravates you

○ You yell or become irate at other drivers

Sleep

○ You have difficulty falling sleep

○ Your mind starts working, remembering, planning, worrying

○ You wake up or can't get to sleep because you are concerned, worried or anxious

○ You have nightmares

Energetic Pick-ups

○ You lack energy or feel lethargic

○ You have caffeinated or sweet drinks, nicotine, alcohol, soda, candy or other sweets

○ You are a risk taker

○ Your job or hobbies scare others

○ You are a harsh taskmaster, driving yourself endlessly to work or to be of service to anyone who needs you

○ You are addicted to drama

○ You have affairs or multiple partners

○ You are flirtatious

○ You often begin and end friendships and intimate relationships

○ You are often arguing, accusing, placing blame on others

If you find yourself reflected in this list and *are not* on a path towards change, a domino effect that brings you to physical and spiritual imbalance, illness, and then crisis is only a matter of time.

Rather than being at the whim of a dynamic that shifts our physical and emotional health this way and that, we need to realize that health is not only a state of being, it is also a way of life. We must each be responsible for the constant tending, shaping and nurturing of our own environments and ecosystems.

Nurture and invite calm.

Notice your life, what you are doing, not doing, and who you are with when any of the above energetic disruptions occur. This is the time for internal spring cleaning and no one can clean your house for you. Rearrange the furniture by taking out the stimulants and the downers and inviting new guests: people, places, activities, emotions, etc., that are inspiring, grounded, joyful and calm. As you invite these in, you will find yourself under their compelling and magical influence.

Change comes fast once you take an active role, if you make *choices* towards calm states of mind and body.

Resources: Watch Dr. Paul H. Brenner, *Epigenetics and the Space Around Us* on Ted.com.

 *Practice Session 6*

Unpacking Your Luggage

For this practice, you will need a piece of paper, colored pencils or crayons.

Phase 1

Write the following words:

- Throat
- Jaw
- Forehead
- Neck
- Heart
- Back
- Stomach
- Shoulders
- Head

Close your eyes and scan each of these areas of your body. Pair up the emotion listed below that dwells in the areas listed above:

- Sadness
- Anger
- Irritation
- Loss

Feel free to add other emotions or parts of the body.

Looking at each body part and each emotion, ask yourself:

- How much space does the emotion take up?
- What shape is it?
- What color is it?
- Are they dense, muddy, foggy, clear, opaque, dry, whirling or turbulent, calm or serene?

Your answers may come to you in a flash or take a few moments to appear.

Phase 2

Draw a map of yourself using the paper and colored pencils or crayons.

Draw a basic outline of a person. This requires *no* artistic skills at all; you just need a very basic and rudimentary representation. Using the colored pencils or crayons, draw in the shapes and colors. If words come to you that are connected to these forces, these weather and land patterns, within you, write them in.

Your goal is to be able to see the forces within you, to look inside the heavy suitcase you've been lugging around. As you see this extra weight, ask yourself if any of it is outdated, unnecessary or useless.

Phase 3

Imagine unburdening yourself, unloading the suitcase, one item at a time.

Albert Einstein said, *"Imagination is everything. It is the preview of life's coming attractions."*

Use your meditation skills to return to a lighter version of yourself, as you let go of each piece of your luggage. Imagine and contemplate what this lighter version of you could do, and who you could be.

Use EFT to clear the energetics of the heaviness you have been carrying.

Practice Session 7

Breaking Patterns: Stop, Look, Go

Stop, Look, Go

Brother David Steindle-Rast says, "Stop, Look, Go." *Stop* what you are doing and saying, even for a moment. If you can *stop*, you will *look* at what is around and within you and then *go* forward once you have your moment of clarity and choice.

At **any** point you can *stop, look* and then *go*, changing gears and switching tracks. It's never too late, but you will have to remind yourself that you can and must choose to go through each of these steps, and practice many times over.

Pattern Inheritance: These inheritances are upon us before we know it, pre-thought, instinctual patterns that are unplanned. For many it was something we woke up to when we stepped into our life and only catch glimpses of when we see the marks we carry and the marks we've left on others. Some welcome these patterns and may even be proud of them, wanting and needing them for their connection to family or the past. Others rage against them, and this too ensures connection.

With needle
and thread,
we have
painstakingly sewn
our own pattern.
Now, let us painstakingly undo
who we are,
who we have been,
and what has held us together.

Carefully cut the thread and dismantle the illusion.
We will not collapse.
Like a kite that floats in the breeze,
we can and will rise.

We are strong,
stronger than we know,
stronger than we ever imagined.
Our strength spans eternities
and comes from being one
with the currents of life,
rising and falling, floating and
drifting into new kingdoms,
reconnecting to the kingdom within.

It is because we don't know who we are,

because we are unaware that the Kingdom of Heaven is here within us,

that we behave in the generally silly,

the often insane,

the sometimes criminal ways that are so characteristically human.

ALDOUS HUXLEY
THE PERENNIAL PHILOSOPHY

Phase 1

Stop and Look for symptoms of Pattern Inheritance:

- A feeling that you're not living or expressing the life that's inside *you*

- Forcing a smile on your face

- Feeling that you're "happy enough" but believing you can't feel joy

- You're uncomfortable within your body, feel stuck, irritated

- Feeling jailed in yourself or your life

- Holding your body very tight all the time

- Wondering, "Why did I say/do that?" or "Where did that come from?"

- Wanting to take back something you said or did

- Wishing you hadn't responded in the same way and wondering why you can't do it differently

- Being told some version of "You sound just like your mother when you're upset!"

- Wanting to change but can't see how that can happen, maybe you've tried but you keep falling back on old habits and patterns

- Believing you were always who you are right now and don't remember ever being or feeling different

My simple recipe for a joyful day is this: Stop and wake up; look and be aware of what you see; then go on with all the alertness you can muster for the opportunity the moment offers. Looking back in the evening, on a day on which I made these three steps over and over, is like looking at an apple orchard heavy with fruit.

BROTHER DAVID STEINDLE-RAST
WWW.GRATEFULNESS.ORG

Phase 2

Take out photos of your family and yourself, both old and recent.

Look for the similarities between yourself and your family. Notice facial expressions, posture and emotions (expressed or unexpressed). Ask yourself if you have the same physical ailments (headaches, fatigue), physical habits (crack your knuckles, yawn when you're uncomfortable), tend towards the same set of emotions (anger, depression, irritation) or if you use the same words, verbal expressions or tone of voice.

Make a list of the habits, behaviors, emotions, beliefs and patterns you inherited.

Emotions: Are there similarities in how you express your emotions? Think about when you are sad, angry, bewildered or in any other emotional state.

Behaviors: Are you stubborn, controlling, jealous, mean, a hoarder or selfish? Who in your family do you take after? Behavioral patterns often reveal themselves when we are hungry or tired. Notice what you gravitate towards. Look at food and drink choices and what you do (go for a run or to the gym, watch TV). Notice if being tired or hungry affects your behavior (getting easily irritated or impatient), or your emotions (depressed or upset). Does anyone else you grew up with respond in the same way? Behaviors are often emotions in action, and both the emotion and the behavior may be inherited patterns.

Beliefs: Who shares your beliefs and opinions? Start with the most obvious topics: religion, politics, relationships, food and the environment. It's fine to hold the same beliefs but you don't want to think they are your own if they are not. If you have held a belief that you realize you don't really care about or know enough about, let it go.

Phase 3

Go towards transformation.

Once you realize your responses may be habitual and inherited, you can make a choice to disinherit and find your own way. *Stopping* and *Looking* gives us the choice of how we *Go* forward. When you find yourself playing out an inherited pattern, *Stop* and *Go* in a different direction, re-writing the script. Return to this like a mantra. **Stop. Look** at the pattern. **Go** forward by changing course. It takes practice to create a healthier, more meaningful and more authentic life, but it also takes practice to learn to speak, walk and ride a bike. This path is one of working with more than the fundamental tools we need to survive.

The road may seem long, but it is probably the same length whichever direction we go in. We all walk this path, why not *Stop, Look* and *Go* on one that leads to a better life?

Do not think this path is the path of passivity. You must be attentive and listen.

FAOUZI SKAALI

Find Your Compelling Vision

Who we know ourselves to be is based on our history of actions, events and behaviors, on what others have come to expect of us *and* on what we have come to expect of ourselves. It can be difficult to let go, change or transform because we feel we are locked in to this path or story that has solidified around and within us. Often, instead of growing up, we grow old, not solving our problems, just becoming accustomed to them, drawing them in to the folds of our body, so they become the fabric of our life.

For this practice, you will need the following:

- a pen
- a roll of blank paper or a number of pieces of large paper taped together
- your journal

Phase 1

Create a storyboard of your life. List the events and experiences that have been the markers of your life. Put these down in a linear fashion, moving through time from early in your life to later, as if it were the storyboard for a movie.

Scan your memories for anything that has been influential or impactful: people, places, events and situations. This map can begin at birth and ends in, or close to, the present time. What do you remember that was eventful, a turning point or had an impact, good or bad?

Once you have finished, spend some time with it objectively. What do you think of the *person* who has led this life? What do you think of the *life* you have led? Have you created the life you want for yourself? How does this sit with you? Are you pleased, excited, horrified? See your life thus far as a movie, the movie of *your* life. Without intervention, ponder its natural course, who this person will become and how they will live their life.

Phase 2

Now you have come to the fork in the road of the storyline. First, create the path that reflects the worst of all possible outcomes. Tell the story, writing it down as a continuation of your life.

Next, create the story of what we'll call your *Compelling Vision*, the best possible life and version of yourself. Allow your mind to roam freely and your desires, hopes and dreams to be expressed.

Now is not the time to confine yourself to perceived or actual limitations, such as taking care of a child or an elderly relative, or feeling that you cannot leave your present job or that you are too old to do what you truly want.

Phase 3

In your journal, create a list, a plan—all the steps to be taken to achieve your Compelling Vision.

This phase is a brain dump, writing anything that comes to mind that needs to be done to get you from here to there. By allowing yourself to begin, you are already taking the first steps to creating this vision; you are already on your way.

After the brain dump, you can organize your steps into a timeline and begin your journey to your Compelling Vision.

Phase 4

Go public by describing your Compelling Vision to someone. Your vision and its path will be more powerful and direct if it's not a private one. If you do not have someone to share it with, begin to create an environment of like-minded people, people who have similar life visions and callings. What type of people would support your vision and where could you meet them?

 *Practice Session 9*

Find Your Neutral

Finding Neutral works towards an actual change in the chemistry of our brains (decreasing cortisol, the 'stress hormone' and adrenalin, the 'fight or flight hormone'), and therefore plays an instrumental role in our transformation process.

Neutral is a place within that is calm and at peace, where there are no external or internal disruptions. Unfortunately, it is the other moments that often claim our attention and remain with us for hours, days, and even years.

Most of us habitually disregard or minimize the importance of this state of Neutral. We see these moments of calm as fleeting visitors over whose comings and goings we have no control. By gently noticing and placing subtle attention on these precious and vital moments of calm and peace, we honor their presence and cultivate their return.

Phase 1

To find Neutral, remind yourself of a time or moment when your mind and body were calm and felt at peace.

These moments may occur when you are doing something you love ... going for a walk or a run, being creative, enjoying the stars or a sunset. Maybe it's when you first wake or during your morning shower, while you are stretching, having breakfast or during a meditation practice.

Now that you have this memory, place your noticing on the state of calm you experience rather than the activity that produces it. Invite this state of calm to stay with you and notice when your state shifts and what takes it away.

Phase 2

Cultivate Neutral. Our busy lives don't encourage us to bask in a state of calm, but this is exactly what we need to do. Close your eyes and allow yourself to experience it again. In this way you can keep coming back to it. For some, music helps them find this place, but just keep in the mind that the place you are shifting to is within you. You are practicing *shifting within yourself.*

When you realize you have moved away from your state of calm and peace, like a meditation, notice what pulls you away and where you are pulled to (feeling that you need to get on with your day, excitement, anxiety, preoccupation, grumpiness, impatience, frustration, anger, happiness, or sadness).

This will take active and conscious effort. You may not always accomplish your goal but the more you practice, the more achievable it will become. The next practice, Coming Back to Neutral, builds on this and will strengthen your shifting and awareness skills.

 *Practice Session 10*

Coming Back to Neutral

Coming Back to Neutral trains us to quickly notice an emotional shift out of Neutral and increases our familiarity and ease with shifting back into it. Knowing we *can shift* back and *deciding* to do so, rather than remaining at the mercy of our emotions, brings equilibrium to our life's path.

On the Dual Path, we treat ourselves and others with honor and respect, valuing both body and spirit and the connection between the two. If we do not periodically bring ourselves back to Neutral, this is simply not a reality that is within our grasp. Instead, our habits and emotions run riot over our lives and the lives of those around us.

Emotions, while natural and human, must be recognized for what they are; either an old pattern or a call to action, to take time for ourselves, to make changes in our life or to let go. Because emotions usually go unattended to, just like thought, there is often a build-up of suppressed and unexpressed emotion. We often don't notice our own shifts into anger or irritation until there is chaos, hurt or damage, and when we do notice it is often once we are already out of control, and have spontaneously erupted. In this unstable state, we have a tendency to move from one emotion to the next, moving further and further off our Path.

For this practice, you will need 3 chairs.

Place two chairs facing each other, and the third chair facing these two. Keep a fourth on hand.

Phase 1

Using Practice Session # 9, find Neutral. Sit down in one of the two chairs that are facing each other. This is now your Neutral Chair and you can only sit here if you are in Neutral. Spend as long as you need in this chair, becoming familiar with yourself in Neutral, noticing, how you feel, your body posture, expression and voice.

Phase 2

Now make a conscious effort to conjure up something that will take you out of Neutral. As soon as you are no longer in Neutral move to the opposite chair. Being out of Neutral can be as simple as feeling out of sorts, feeling ungrounded, or it may be an emotion such as anger or sadness.

Label this chair the Sadness Chair or the Feeling Out of Sorts Chair, etc. Now that you're in this chair, notice any changes in your facial expression, posture or in how you feel.

Phase 3

Look back at the Neutral Chair and see yourself as you were in Neutral, noticing your posture, how you breathe, look and feel in Neutral. Compare this with your present state.

Phase 4

1. Move to the third chair, the In Between Chair. From this chair look over at yourself in each of the two chairs, noticing differences in facial expression, body posture and language.

Observing yourself in this way is powerful in itself.

2. From the In Between Chair, ask what you in the Neutral chair have to say to you in the opposite chair? Move to the Neutral Chair and say it. Once you have said it, move to the opposite chair and notice your reaction. If a dialogue begins, allow it, switching to whichever chair you are speaking from. Move to the In Between chair whenever you want to witness, step back and observe.

Fully notice yourself in each chair. Notice your facial expression, tone of voice, body posture (leaning forward or back...), tightness, tension, and sense of openness or closed-ness in your body, how and if your arms and hands move as you talk, etc.

3. Even if you don't have a dialogue, move back and forth from Neutral to the opposite chair, noticing as you switch, what changes in you when you begin to slip out of neutral and how long it takes for those changes to occur. ·

Notice that you can do it, that Neutral is right there, within you and within your reach. All you have to do is become familiar with it and make the choice to move into it.

Phase 5

This phase converts the skill of Coming Back to Neutral from a fixed arena, using the chairs, into your daily life. Whenever you find you have drifted out of Neutral, use this practice. The more you Come Back to Neutral the more you will manifest a calm, stable and centered self.

Choose a word that describes the movement of one state of mind to another. From now on, at the moment you recognize that you are moving into an old state of mind or emotion, you can say this word to yourself and move to Neutral.

My word is 'switch'—it makes me think of railroad tracks. The track I want to switch to has become increasingly familiar and switching takes less and less time and effort.

Please note: This practice is not about denying our feelings; it's about not being at the mercy of emotional and behavioral patterns, about finding balance and being able to make a choice.

If a feeling or state of mind seems very familiar, it's probably an old pattern, something that has run its course.

Inhalations and Exhalations

This path we are on is a journey of Exhaling, of letting go, an emptying of all we have Inhaled, all our identities, those we claim for ourselves and those that others claim for us. Without this practice, we are chiseled in stone, our story written and told and laid out before us, with no room for change and no room for growth.

What is the self we are identified with, that of our own making or choosing or due to the perceptions of others? While we may think of ourselves in one way, others may have a different perception of us altogether. These perceptions may be based on one event or incident, on the past or the present, one that you either embraced or have been trying to shake off.

There is no right or wrong perception; after all, it is perception. True, past, present or perceived: it doesn't matter because our path is set towards transformation.

We strive to create
a whole,
not realizing that wholeness
does not come from
ethnicity, religion, or
relationships
and is not disrupted
by a misspent youth,
bad choices,
trauma,
parents,
or by any other force.

Wholeness is arrived at through
deep inhalations
of all the elements that have
made us who we are,
and deep exhalations,
letting them,
and what we know of ourselves
go again.

In this list of common inhalations, put an M (for 'me'), on those words that _you_ feel describe you and an O (for 'others') on those words _others_ would use to describe you. You may have words marked with both M's and O's and others with neither.

__ Accepting	__ Curious	__ Gross	__ Loner	__ Predictable	__ Subservient
__ Afraid	__ Dark	__ Grouchy	__ Lost	__ Private	__ Successful
__ Aggressive	__ Daring	__ Grounded	__ Loud	__ Professional	__ Survivor
__ Androgynous	__ Delicate	__ Guilt-ridden	__ Loved	__ Quiet	__ Talented
__ Angry	__ Dependable	__ Handsome	__ Lovely	__ Realist	__ Thrifty
__ Anxious	__ Dependent	__ Hard Worker	__ Loving	__ Reliable	__ Thoughtful
__ Artificial	__ Direct	__ Hardened	__ Masculine	__ Resourceful	__ Thoughtless
__ Artistic	__ Directed	__ Happy	__ Mature	__ Responsible	__ Thought-
__ Asexual	__ Disconnected	__ Hardy	__ Mean	__ Restless	Provoking
__ Awkward	__ Distracted	__ Healthy	__ Mediator	__ Rich	__ Tidy
__ Beautiful	__ Dreamer	__ Hero	__ Misfit	__ Risk Taker	__ Touchy Feely
__ Boring	__ Dutiful	__ Honorable	__ Motherly	__ Ruthless	__ Trustworthy
__ Bully	__ Dynamic	__ Hopeful	__ Muscular	__ Sadistic	__ Unavailable
__ Calm	__ Emotional	__ Hurtful	__ Natural	__ Scattered	__ Uncaring
__ Candid	__ Energetic	__ Immature	__ Negative	__ Self Centered	__ Unemotional
__ Caring	__ Extravagant	__ Impatient	__ Nice	__ Self-Confident	__ Ungrounded
__ Charming	__ Failure	__ Incompetent	__ Nonconformist	__ Selfish	__ Unhealthy
__ Challenging	__ Feminine	__ Independent	__ Obedient	__ Sensitive	__ Uninvolved
__ Charismatic	__ Fit	__ Indifferent	__ Obstinate	__ Serious	__Unpredictable
__ Childish	__ Flaky	__ Influential	__ Offensive	__ Severe	__Unreserved
__ Childlike	__ Flexible	__ Innocent	__ Old Fashioned	__ Sexual	__ Untidy
__ Clumsy	__ Foolish	__ Insecure	__ Out of Control	__ Sexy	__ Vicious
__ Compassionate	__ Forgetful	__ Inspiring	__ Passionate	__ Shopaholic	__ Victim
__ Competent	__ Frail	__ Jaded	__ Patient	__ Skittish	__ Visionary
__ Complainer	__ Friendly	__ Jealous	__ Personable	__ Slutty	__ Volatile
__ Conformist	__ Fun	__ Joyful	__ Philosophical	__ Soulful	__ Weak
__ Contemplative	__ Funny	__ Judgmental	__ Plain	__ Smothering	__ Wise
__ Controlling	__ Generous	__ Kind	__ Positive	__ Spacey	__ Wonderful
__ Crazy	__ Gossipy	__ Lazy	__ Possessive	__ Spiritual	__ Workaholic
__ Creative	__ Graceful	__ Leader	__ Powerful	__ Strong	__ Worried
__ Cruel	__ Grieving	__ Lonely	__ Playful	__ Stubborn	__ Wuss

Phase 2

Take your list of Inhalations and write a 'Y' (Yes) next to the positive ones you either want to keep or cultivate. Write a 'N' (No) for the negatives you choose to discard.

Now take the specific words, and write each one on a piece of paper, keeping the 'Y' and 'N' piles separate.

Phase 3

Take the pile of Yes words and set them out in front of you in a section of their own, on your *left*. Do the same to the No pile, placing them on your *right*. Do not place them the other way round.

As you scan the words in the Yes pile on the left, Inhale deeply. Then move your gaze to the pile on your right and Exhale deeply as you scan those words. Do this three times. Now take one word from each pile and Inhale one from the Yes pile and Exhale one from the No pile, working your way through your pile of words.

While your breath should be relaxed, breathe as loudly and fully as you can, breathing in and out of your mouth.

Exhale,
Again
and Again and
Again

Because if we only inhale
what has been given to us,
we fill up, and fill up
until there is no longer room
for who we are.

It is the exhale that is important,
as if jumping off a cliff
into nothingness.
— a flight into a deep, open
and expansive self
with eyes wide open
and wings spread so perfectly
that every breeze that floats
through them
can be savored.

Each breath is a new beginning in your body.

Breathing is a cornerstone to the quantity of your energy, and the quality of your life.

Changing your relationship to your breathing—from unconscious or second nature to conscious and intentional—can dramatically change your overall health and vitality.

For all of us, our breath is crucial to each moment of our being.

NAOMI SOPHIA CALL
FOUNDATION OF YOUTH EXERCISES

Find the Force Within

From the moment we are born, we are students of life, learning about right and wrong, good and bad. Our exposure to the difficulties and struggles of the world (Earth) often overwhelms our highly sensitive systems, until suddenly one day we realize we are lost.

How Are You Lost?

• A personal injury attorney gets so drunk that he shouldn't drive home, but he does.

• A woman struggling with her husband and children lusts after the butcher, the baker and the candlestick maker, plus the gardener.

• A man goes through a painful divorce and threatens his spouse.

• The single woman who chooses the same addictive personality, again and again and again and wonders why she is in her 50's and still hasn't found the right man.

• A self-proclaimed happily married man who lusts after his daughter's eighteen-year-old friends.

• The woman who wants her life to change but is unwilling to make any changes.

• The man who carries the world on his shoulders, who is so bitter about his lot in life, it's all he can talk about.

• The woman who is compassionate, caring, giving and supportive, or maybe feels obligated, who gives and gives to work, friends, family, to everyone, and doesn't understand why she is sick or unhappy.

There are times throughout our lives when we are supposed to get lost. These times are vital opportunities to grow towards wisdom. We get lost so we can find a better version of ourselves. It's not such a bad thing.

We get lost when our children leave home, when we divorce, when we are widowed, when we lose or quit a job, starve ourselves or stuff ourselves, have an argument, lose our temper, feel frustrated, panicky, or angry are tight, in pain or injured are sick, can't sleep, have a headache, turn on the TV, when, yet again, we do the same thing that we've been meaning to change – get drunk, have sex with someone because we're bored or need excitement, – eat that bagel that's become a morning habit – or the pizza that's become our evening habit, – find ourselves in the same unsatisfying or abusive relationship...

We are in the liquid stage of internal reorganization when we recognize the connection between action and feeling, feeling and the need to contemplate, when we give up fear so we can boldly go in the direction our inherent wisdom is driving us towards.

- The woman who gets into yet another relationship with someone who is already in a relationship.
- The man who has no goals, no ambitions, no direction, who cannot make a decision, who does not know which way to go.
- The person who cannot be at a social gathering, large or small, without a drink in hand.
- The person who flirts to feel they are attractive; to connect, make an impression, feel good about themself or to get what they want.
- The person who feels lost, has panic attacks, nightmares, or who cannot sleep.
- Type A personalities, the control freak who needs to have the dishes washed just the way they want, who feels that "to do it right" they need to do it themselves.
- The person who goes to yoga classes, but loses control with their children, drives too fast or is hot-tempered.

Phase 1

Begin a list in your journal as you recognize the ways you are, or have been, lost. These times, which happen at various junctures in our lives, are potential turning points. The turning point is meant as an opportunity for growth. If we ignore the opportunity we stunt our growth, distort our true nature, and crush the spirit that is propelling us ahead. In time, we lose faith in ourselves, our heart feels injured, and we close and protect rather than open, grow and strengthen towards our true potential.

Rather than letting history become our present and our future, we need to take a hand in shaping ourselves and nurturing our growth in the direction of our inherent wisdom.

Many of us ignore the signs of how we are lost, berate ourselves or try and do things differently. The Dual Path is to connect to our inherent wisdom.

Phase 2

Read the following words aloud, pausing to allow each word to have its own sense of space as you sense how it resonates within you:
- Compassion
- Love
- Presence
- Gratitude
- Growth
- Wisdom
- Peace
- Meaning

There is an inherent force within each of us which propels us forward towards the light (Heaven). This force is encapsulated by one of the words above, one word that will resonate more strongly or deeply than the others. Find yours.

The difficulties, challenges and pressures of life can easily distract from the force within, and even make us forget it existed in the first place. Yet this force lives at the core of our being.

Your life may or may not yet reflect this quality, but it has been there somewhere, pulling you forward or pushing you from behind, an invisible force reminding you of your own deep sense of truth.

Look for the one that has served to guide you; that you have in some way, subtly or obviously, dedicated your life and your heart to. Contemplate how the exploration and lessons of this force has expressed itself in your life, and what you have learned.

Phase 3

Find your mantra below, and then close your eyes and repeat it, allowing it to soak in and resonate on a cellular level.

I am Compassionate; I am Compassion

I am Loving; I am Love

I am Present; I am Presence

I am Grateful; I am Gratitude

I am Growing; I am Growth

I am Wise; I am Wisdom

I am Peaceful; I am Peace

I am Meaningful; I am Meaning

Now sit in meditation, using these words as your silent mantra, repeating it again and again. When you notice you are no longer doing so, just bring yourself back to it.

Practice Slowness

Many of us want a long life, yet we move through the one we have as fast as we can. We think that if we do it fast we can do more, and then we'll be able to move on to the next thing. Often, 'the next thing' isn't what we really want to be doing either, so we do that as fast as we can too. Speed is a habit and an addiction.

With our daily responsibilities and to-do lists, there is no doubt the 'fast setting' can be useful. However, rather than using it as a tool, many of us get stuck in fast mode and allow it to dictate *everything* we do.

This practice resets your speed setting by working with the automatic things you do.

Phase 1

Practice the following right now. Explore how slowly you can:

- Inhale and exhale
- Say your name
- Stand up
- Sit down
- Walk from one room to another

Take it to the extreme and drastically slow each thing down. It's easy and natural to have fun with these, but stay grounded and in your center as you go through the list several times.

As you move through the next few days, explore doing the following *slowly*:

- **Wash the dishes.** Do this slowly and calmly. See if you can take pleasure in the skillful movement of your hands as they coordinate this dance.
- **Wake up and get out of bed.** Notice the time between sleep and wakefulness, that drowsy, relaxed state we can learn so much from.
- **Brush your teeth.** Many people are over vigor-

She tells me
she has had
so much to do,
she has been doing everything
as fast as she can:
getting in and out of her car,
eating, walking, talking, washing dishes....
She is an adrenalin rush in full army dress,
an accident waiting to happen,
chronic fatigue winding its way
into her life and heart,
an illness of mind and body taking hold.

If we come to know ourselves
as a bundle of stress,
traveling through our lives with
no time to breathe
or look around,
traveling faster than a speeding train,
then we may not want to interrupt the flow
or change the way we function.
If the only speed setting we have is fast,
the very thought of being calm within
may also cause us to feel panicky within.

ous because they don't really pay attention. Notice in what order you go through this ritual and if you turn the water on before you actually need it.

- **Eat.** Notice if you go for the next mouthful of food before you've finished chewing what you already have. Practice putting your utensils down while you are chewing and only picking them up when your mouth is empty and you are ready for more.

- **Dressing and undressing.** As you slip you arms into sleeves, legs into pants or skirts, feet into shoes, slippers or sandals, notice the movement of your body, the exact moment of contact and the feel of that contact with your body. Notice any changes as each part of your body is dressed.

- **Get in and out of your car.** Try to do this gently rather than throwing your stuff in and slamming the door.

A river caresses the rocks, the sun, the trees, each and every time. Caress the moments you typically don't notice, and even those you consider boring or a waste of time. Every moment is a moment of your life. Don't try to fast-forward through any of them.

Keep coming back to this slowness. It is the application that is vital. As you stray, bring yourself back. Notice if you feel irritated, pent-up, outside your center or manic, and find your way back to Neutral.

Resources: Try the Feldenkrais Method or the Alexander Technique for more exploration through bodywork.

For inspiration, watch the movie, *Click* with Adam Sandler or Eckhart Tolle's books and DVD's.

 *Practice Session 14*

Honoring Yourself

There are a great number of obstacles to honoring our selves, and a great number of rewards. Honoring Yourself is an *attitude*, one that is seen by some as radical.

Honoring Yourself means being true to *yourself* as you embrace your decisions, strengths and powers on this journey within. It allows us to move forward without shame or guilt, tied only to what we know to be true.

There are times of our life when this is particularly challenging, such as when to honor the self means a departure from what is expected or required of us:

- When our heart tells us to go in a certain direction in life that others do not support us on or see the value of

- When we fall in love with someone our family doesn't approve of
- When we don't carry the same beliefs as those around us
- When we transition from seeing ourselves as part of a group such as supporters of a particular sports team, patriotic, belonging to a political party, or tied to a gender identity or sexual orientation and enter into a deeper and more complete manifestation of ourselves.

Under the weight of the fear of being different or wrong we may compromise, play it safe, do as we're told, try to fit in or be crippled by the need for acceptance.

We crave a sense of belonging, which for many is enough to give us an identity, to know what to believe and how to act and behave but it is a compromise, not an honoring of the unique spirit that is yours.

However, our lives are not arrows with which we get one shot. We are on a pathway, meandering forward, embracing first our spirit, and then our options and opportunities.

We must learn to honor ourselves, give ourselves permission to honor ourselves, and we must continue doing so throughout our life.

What is the self,
if not precious,
fragile and temporary?
We cannot give away
our dreams and aspirations
and hope to be happy, satisfied and real.
We cannot be disappointed by our choices
without being disappointed by ourselves.

Do we think we can do such
dishonor to our spirit,
just do what we are told or
feel a responsibility to,
and still be vital in energy
let alone a
warm,
trusting,
caring,
intelligent,
thoughtful,
peaceful being?

A writing practice

- How do you feel about the idea of honoring yourself? Does it feel appealing or foreign?
- What does it mean to honor *yourself* and still be caring, compassionate and responsive to others?
- How do you honor yourself?
- How don't you honor yourself? What gets in the way, what are your battles and obstacles?
- How do you give up on yourself?
- What are you doing instead?
- What fears emerge when you imagine making choices to live *your* life?

Value your growth towards your amazing potential. Honor yourself in your behavior, your choices, how you move consistently towards your dreams. If you find yourself wasting time or giving in to habit, fatigue or pressure, just move yourself back on track. Like a meditation, when you realize you are no longer repeating the mantra or are no longer focused on your breath, bring yourself back.

Obstacles exist only to make us choose the right course, again and again, and again.

 *Practice Session 15*

Be Good

What are you good at?

Find something that has meaning.

Become good

Become great

Take pride

Have pride

Honor your gift

Honor that you are alive

Don't wait until it's half over

and time for a mid-life crisis—

or that it's all over.

Always

live your life well,

with meaning,

honoring its sacredness.

If you slip

moment-to-moment,

day-to-day,

just remind yourself

gently,

to come back to sacredness.

It is amazing how many of us keep ourselves in self-imposed spiritual and emotional prisons. Our souls are not open, but are, rather, closed tightly. Behind those closed doors we keep so many feelings that are instrumental in keeping us at the edge of life instead of being immersed in life, while we yet have the chance. For the longest time, I knew something was off-center in my life, but didn't know what it was ... not until recently. As a child, I didn't feel honored or liked in my family; it seemed that I could never do anything right; I looked funny ... and all that baggage became feelings that I carefully folded and carried around inside me.

Life is a little too short for that.

And so, for the rest of my days, however many those may be, I am going to "walk in myself." I am going to appreciate my gifts and use them, and not worry about what I don't have and what I cannot do. It really doesn't matter. There is plenty I can do ... and will do.

REV. DR. SUSAN K. SMITH
GIRL TALK: HONORING OURSELVES
RETRIEVED FROM HTTP://CANDIDOBSERVA-
TION.WORDPRESS.COM

Phase 1

Make a list of what you do. This may include your work or profession, being a lover, husband, wife, parent, pet owner, sister, brother, friend, volunteer, or whatever else you can think of.

Phase 2

On this list, put an 'M' next to those things you feel you are Master at. To earn an M, you must be actively engaged, pursuing new information on how it is done and asking yourself how you could be doing it better.

Phase 3

Put an 'H' next to those things you do half-heartedly. Ask yourself how important this thing is to you and if you really want to be doing this activity or role. What if you were to drop it completely, just stop? What if you were to put your heart and soul into it?

Phase 4

Being Good requires that your heart is in what you do, so that even in the challenging moments, when you find yourself irritated, annoyed, angry or defensive, you *want* to ask, "Is this as good as I can be in this moment?" Use the skills from Sacred Practice #7 *Breaking Patterns: Stop, Look, Go.* Stop and Look when you notice yourself responding in a way that is not useful, unhealthy an old pattern or simply disconnected or uncaring. Drawing from Practice Session #12, *Find the Force Within*, Go in a different direction by recalling and using the energy of your personal mantra.

A teaching story from the North American Plains Indians tells of a young man who comes to his grandfather and says, "There are two wolves inside me. One wants to kill and destroy, and the other one wants to make peace and bring beauty. Which one will win, Grandfather?" The old man answers, "Whichever one you feed."

ALBERTO VILLOLDO AND DAVID PERLMUTTER, *POWER UP YOUR BRAIN: THE NEUROSCIENCE OF ENLIGHTENMENT*

Be Prepared for Change

She sits on the couch during our check-in,

sipping from a huge cup of coffee she has brought with her to this massage session,

and lists the medications she is on is for her heart palpitations.

She says she could probably get rid of them if she gave up coffee.

She states this with a laugh which pronounces the idea itself as absurd.

"That seems like a fair exchange," I say, looking her in the eyes.

Looking down at her coffee,

she laughs again, nervously,

and adds that there's no guarantee

the palpitations would actually go away

if she were to give up her coffee.

THE DILEMMA

To laugh is to risk appearing a fool.

To weep is to risk appearing sentimental.

To reach out for another is to risk involvement.

To expose feelings is to risk rejection.

To place your dreams before the crowd is to risk ridicule.

To love is to risk not being loved in return.

To go forward in the face of overwhelming odds is to risk failure.

But risks must be taken,

because the greatest hazard in life is to risk nothing.

The person who risks nothing does nothing, has nothing, is nothing.

He may avoid suffering and sorrow,

but he cannot learn, feel, change, grow or love.

Chained by his certitudes, he is a slave.

He has forfeited his freedom.

UNKNOWN AUTHOR

Being Prepared for Change is a contemplative practice. Sit with each question or statement and notice your thoughts, emotions and reaction. To which of the following do you say Yes, No or Maybe? Which makes you uncomfortable, determined, or hopeful?

- Do you have a belief system that says you should not or cannot change? Are you willing to explore where your belief comes from? Are you willing to let it go? Change is a natural and integral part of life, essential to growth and maturity.

- Can you allow yourself to be a naturally and constantly transmuting organism, constantly coming into being?

- Are you open and willing to go in any direction that is the right one for you?

- Would you go in a direction even though you don't know where it leads?

- Even if you were afraid, would you go forward anyway?

- Take an honest look at your way of being, behavior, reactions, thought and emotional landscape, and set yourself on a better course.

For inspiration, read, *Why Your Life Sucks* by Alan Cohen, *The Hero Within* by Carol Pearson and *King, Warrior, Magician, Lover* by Robert Moore and Douglas Gillette.

Are you willing to:

- Have a different life? That may mean a different town, landscape, partner, or lifestyle?

- Not "make-do"?

- Be soft and pliable on this journey, as well as resolute?

- Prioritize yourself?

- Dedicate time to do your practices?

- Change how you look and dress to express your spirit and true nature? An awakened spirit cannot bear to be masked with make-up or hair coloring. Unfortunately, many come to believe they are the people who wear the masks, and have no sense of a true and deeper self-worth and being. Are you willing to go deep, to be deep?

- Drink enough water for your body? What about the inconvenience of going to the bathroom more frequently? Many of us go on diets to cleanse our systems of toxins. Water in, water and toxins out. Most of us just need to go to the bathroom more often. For inspiration read, *Your Body's Many Cries for Water* by F. Batmanghelidj, M.D. or visit watercure.com.

All you need to do
is change something in your life
and then follow the yellow brick road
for your life's path to unravel.

It is the unraveling we are afraid of.
Where does it end?
Is there a map?
We have no guarantees
and not even a vision to aspire to.

Of course there are those who are
primed for this turn of events,
and those for whom the turn
has already happened
— soul mates in a vast
universe of living.

- Change your diet? Eat more greens and fruit? For inspiration read Kris Carr's *Crazy, Sexy Diet* and *Crazy, Sexy Kitchen.*

- Give up coffee, cigarettes, soda, alcohol, whatever your addictions are, and deal with the withdrawal that comes afterwards?

- Surround yourself with people who are supportive of your journey?

- Distance yourself from anyone around you who is abusive, an active alcoholic or drug abuser, a gambler, a sex-addict, untrustworthy, controlling, full of rage or hot tempered, absent, greedy, uncaring, inconsiderate? Does any of this describe who you are?

- Distance yourself from friends who are no longer friends, people who take advantage of you, who don't appreciate you, whose way of life or being isn't supportive or akin to yours. If it no longer feels right, if you feel you are just fulfilling an obligation by spending time with them, let it go.

- Practice being present? Look at the person you are in conversation with. See their eyes, their face. Too often we avoid ourselves and others by not looking, and we miss an awful lot of connection and information, particularly with someone we are close to. Listen to their words. It is easy when we know someone well to think we know exactly what they will say and tune out. Tune in and go deeper into the present. Take some time to look, really look at the movement of a tree branches and leaves in the wind or the rain. Just stay there and look. We tend to operate as if the big spans of time give our lives shape and meaning, such as 'going to work,' and 'coming home', when it's the small things that make a life, and that make a life whole. Being present slows you down, brings you into that very moment of your life. For inspiration, read the introduction to *How to Use Your Eyes*, by James Elkins.

- Practice being considerate and caring? What can you do to make the person you're with feel more relaxed and cared for? If you have gone through the step of distancing yourself from those you shouldn't be around, you will find yourself surrounded by those you really care about. You will want them to feel their best, to feel loved, cared for and supported. You will want them to succeed, to feel confident, relaxed, seen and heard. How do you not support this? What else should you be doing? How else can you be present for them? For inspiration, read, *Soul Mates* by Thomas Moore. If you have found yourself alone, you have a clean canvas to work with.

Your Heavenly Tool Box

Our physical, *Earthly* environment is a reflection and support for our spiritual and Heavenly path and can serve as a signpost constantly pointing us in the right.

Think of this not as a check-list, but as a tool box that sparks the fire of your spirit.

Internals

- You have a regular meditation practice.
- Smiling on the inside has become a habit. You remember to do so the moment you feel off balance.
- You notice when you are not in Neutral, and make the choice to return to it.
- You breathe in what you want to keep, and exhale what you don't.
- You Stop, Look and Go
- You are committed to the Force within.
- You notice what has a positive, uplifting impact, what is neutral and what is negative. You are committed to having a positive impact.
- You honor yourself and at the same time are generous, loving and compassionate.

Your Time

- You have exchanged activities you were doing for ones that are aligned with your path.
- You no longer do things that lack meaning, feel empty, or like a waste of time.
- You are not looking back, but moving forward.
- You make conscious choices around speed.

Your Space

- You have removed what is no longer aligned with who you are becoming and have made choices around every picture on the wall, curtain, rug, bed sheet and cover, lamp, clothing, etc.
- Your garage, basement or attic is clear and you do not have a storage unit.
- You have rearranged your furniture to create a sense of space and to honor what is important.
- You have bought, scanned or copied images that feel sacred and that support your journey, and they are on regular display. Even if you don't know what they mean or represent, you recognize they have a positive impact, that they have touched your soul.

- When you walk into any and every one of your living spaces, you feel good. The colors, sense of space, decorations all reflect the calmer life you are nurturing, a life of spirit, aspirations and growth.

People in Your Life:

- The people you choose to spend time with are also on their path.
- There is a sense of mutual support and understanding.
- Your partner enhances your path. For more on this subject, go to *Partnering on The Dual Path* in Part 5.

For some, having children is a spiritual path, while for others, it's a distraction. Because a parent is necessarily occupied with the many tasks involved with the caretaking of a new human being, for many parents it tends to be the latter rather than the former. However, there are great resources like the books mentioned below for those who seek an integrated spiritual and parenting path. If you are still in the decision stage, and want to be fully committed to a spiritual path, please do it carefully: after all, even Buddha had to leave his family to follow his own path. Whichever camp you are in, the following are good resources:

On Raising Children While on Your Path

- *Planting Seeds: Practicing Mindfulness with Children* by Thich Nhat Hanh
- *The Conscious Parent: Transforming Ourselves, Empowering Our Children* by Dr. Shefali Tsabary.
- *The Mindful Child: How to Help Your Kid Manage Stress and Become Happier, Kinder, and More Compassionate* by Susan Kaiser Greenland.
- *Soul to Soul Parenting: A Guide to Raising a Spiritually Conscious Family* by Annie Burnside.
- *10 Principles for Spiritual Parenting: Nurturing Your Child's Soul* by Mimi Doe.
- *Nurturing Spirituality in Children: Simple Hands-On Activities* by Peggy Jenkins
- *Buddha at Bedtime: Tales of Love and Wisdom for You to Read with Your Child to Enchant, Enlighten and Inspire* by Dharmachari Nagaraja.

On Not Having Children

- *No Kids: 40 Good Reasons Not to Have Children* by Corinne Maier
- *Complete Without Kids: An Insider's Guide to Childfree Living by Choice or by Chance* by Ellen Walker
- *Baby Not on Board: A Celebration of Life without Kids* by Jennifer Shawne

- *No Way Baby!: Exploring, Understanding, and Defending the Decision NOT to Have Children* by Karen Foster
- *Child Free and Loving It!* by Nicki Defago
- *Two Is Enough: A Couple's Guide to Living Childless by Choice* by Laura Scott.

Clear a Path to "You"

A client asks about her sleeping problems.

What can she do?

I ask her to look around my massage room.

She comments on its immediate uplifting and calming effect,

the sense of serenity it gives her.

I tell her that for many, home and work are separate worlds,

while ours are the same,

that both have the same sense of space and serenity.

She looks again, realizing this is not a stage set up for her to step into from time to time;

this is a reality she can create and embrace for herself.

I tell her that each and every thing in this room

not only has a distinct and profound meaning and impact for me,

but that I invite it to have this impact.

Knowing that my surroundings set a tone and infuses me with its energy,

I choose carefully the energy I surround myself with.

I talk about Blane,

making us breakfast that morning,

his face lit up with the beauty of his offering

—the strawberry garnish on top

and how each thing that we choose to surround ourselves with

has a sensibility of its own that we respond to.

I think about my pleasure

each and every time I see Blane,

the light inside my heart.

How when there's a dark cloud hanging over him,

I see and feel that too.

I tell her that we are sensitive beings,

that we need to honor that sensitivity,

that if we inundate ourselves with sensory input

we lose the connection to the energetics of our surroundings,

to their vibrational input.

Look around and see what you have made the center of your world

and what vibrations you are receiving from them.

If they are not aligned with your spirit,

you will not be able to sleep.

If they are not aligned with your spirit,

you cannot move forward on your true path.

You must first clear the path

to allow for forward movement.

The actions of our daily life
like waking, washing, lighting incense
do not seem very important,
but they comprise the whole cosmos.

MASTER TAISEN DESHIMARU

Honoring Our World
or, Super Hero in Action

This last practice completes the cycle as we move from honoring ourselves to honoring our world. Just as Dual Path Meditation moves from an internal practice to one that is fully integrated into our life, the micro to the macro, the Sacred Practices follow the same path.

To do this practice, you will need to have a vision of Heaven and yet be rooted in Earth: this is what the practices have prepared you for.

Remember, we are a complicated, interconnected ecosystem. Our internal world and the world we live in are a Dual Path of their own; when we pollute the waters, the water makes us sick, when we pollute the skies, the skies give us cancer, and when we pollute the food system, we get e-coli. A sick world can never give us a healthy body or mind, and a sick mind can never create a healthy world. In our ecosystem, each is dependent on the other, and together we move forward on our path, towards health or sickness.

The Dual Path means not only that we honor ourselves by Awakening our own Spirit, but that we Honor Our World by protecting that which binds us.

These following steps are relatively small and simple, but a world of individuals doing them can change the world we live in.

Toxic Chemicals
Don't Use Them

Super Hero in Action

Only **you** can make the decision to save your spirit and save the world

On your body: Get to know the Skin Deep website at ewg.org to determine which of the body products you currently use are safe and non-toxic. You can look up *everything*: eye drops, hand sanitizer, toothpaste, deodorant, shampoo, mascara, hair coloring.... to see the level of toxicity and find alternatives. Read, *Toxic Beauty: How Cosmetics and Personal-Care Products Endanger Your Health* by Samuel Epstein and Randall Fitzgerald; *Not Just a Pretty Face: The Ugly Side of the Beauty Industry* by Stacy Malkan; *No More Dirty Looks: The Truth about Your Beauty Products*—and the *Ultimate Guide to Safe and Clean Cosmetics* by Siobhan O'Connor.

In your body: In the U.S. mercury is contained in fillings commonly known as amalgam fillings. The Dr. Oz website says that mercury makes up a full 50% of these fillings. These fillings have been banned in a number of countries due to health and environmental effects. An alternative filling to mercury is ceramic. Read Hal Huggins, *It's All in Your Head*, and *Whole Body Dentistry* by Mark Breiner. Other resources: en.wikipedia.org has information under Dental Amalgam Controversy; search for 'amalgam' on gerson.com and naturalnews.com.

On your lawn or vegetables: Check into organic gardening. Books: *Grow Great Grub: Organic Food for Small Spaces* by Gayla Trail, *Organic Gardening Beginners Manual* by Julie Turner. For eco-friendly and alternatives to lawns: *The Complete Guide to Organic Lawn Care* by Sandy Ann Baker, *The Organic Lawn Care Manual: A Natural, Low-Maintenance System for a Beautiful, Safe Lawn* by Paul Tukey, *Lawn Gone!: Low-Maintenance, Sustainable, Attractive Alternatives for Your Yard* by Pam Penick.

In your house and business: Read *The Non-Toxic Avenger: What You Don't Know Can Hurt You* by Deanna Duke. Use fragrance free, non-chlorine bleach. Use recycled and recyclable or biodegradable paper products such as toilet paper, paper towels and napkins, copy paper, stickies. Change your hand soap, dish soap, laundry soap, all cleaners to a non-toxic product using ewg.org as a guide. Use paint with low or no VOC's, natural insulations, natural fibers for floor coverings, furniture and bedding. Watch the movie: Chemerical.

Set a timer to 5-minutes and walk around your home or office collecting stuff made of plastic. You'll have a pile in less than 3-minutes that would make the plastics industry happy and proud. Watch the movie *Plastic Planet*, read *Plastic-Free: How I Kicked the Plastic Habit and How You Can Too* by Beth Terry and read or listen to *Plastic: A Toxic Love Story* by Susan Freinkel.

Don't use plastic bowls or storage containers or plastic wrap. Buy glass from Kinetic, Pyrex, Libbey. These often come with plastic covers, but the food doesn't usually touch the plastic and the lids are reused again and again, unlike plastic wrap which is used just once and thrown out. Anchor glass refrigerator containers come with glass lids too. Watch *Plastic Planet* and check out these websites: myplasticfreelife.com and lifewithoutplastic.com.

Don't use styrofoam cups. Buy recycled paper ones, or better yet, use ceramic or glass. In an office, require everyone to "bring their own!"

Be water-aware and don't waste it. Watch the movies *Tapped, Flow, Blue Gold* and *Last Call at the Oasis*. Don't buy water in plastic bottles. Buy stainless steel bottles from Klean Kanteen or aquasana.com or glass bottles from aquasana.com and fill them with your own filtered tap water.

Think of *nourishing* your body rather than feeding it.

We know we should eat a healthy breakfast, but what is that? A home-made smoothie full of super foods (foods that have high nutritional content in a small amount of food: goji berries, cocoa powder or nibs, maca, flax seed, chia seeds, etc.) will give your body and mind the energy and alertness it needs. Read: *I Love Green Smoothies* by Katherine Stromick, *Superfoods: The Food and Medicine of the Future* by David Wolfe. On Kindle, *Delicious and Healthy Superfood Breakfasts: Simple, Quick and No-Bake* by Monique Ortega

Buying organic food and limiting your consumption to fresh vegetables and fruit is healthier for the environment and your body and will clean and nourish your system. Add soaked nuts, sprouts, seaweed when you are ready. Read *Crazy, Sexy Diet* and *Crazy, Sexy Kitchen* by Kris Carr. Watch the movies *Food Beware, Food, Inc.* and *Foodmatters.* Alissa Cohen's books are also fabulous, *Living on Live Food* and *Raw Food for Everyone.*

Sprout seeds to put on salads and in smoothies. Sprouts are highly nutritional, low cost and it's good for everyone to be connected with the cycle of growth and nutrition. Make sure you buy organic seeds for sprouting: you don't want to eat pesticide-laden sprouts. There are easy, low-cost systems using pots and lids or glass jars with cheesecloth, or more expensive but vastly less labor intensive automatic sprouters like the Easygreen Sprouter which drains and waters your sprouts for you. Books to consider; *Sprout Garden* by Mark Mathew Braunstein and *Sprouts for the Love of Everybody* by Viktoras Kulvinskas. Websites: sproutpeople.org.

Clear your cupboards and fridge of all processed foods. Watch the movie *Processed People* and read *Real Food Has Curves: How to Get Off Processed Foods, Lose Weight and Love What You Eat* and *Death By Supermarket: The Fattening, Dumbing Down and Poisoning of America* and *Twinkie, Deconstructed: My Journey to Discover How Ingredients in Processed Food are Grown, Mined and Manipulated into What America Eats.*

Eliminate preservatives, sugars, toxins and added hormones in your food—soda, pesticides, chemicals, additives, sugars or sugar substitutes, etc. That means not eating junk food, canned food and most prepared foods. For more information read any raw and living food book and Kris Carr's book *Crazy, Sexy Cancer.* You may not have

We cannot feed ourselves toxic images, behavior, food, cosmetics, and ideas without then becoming toxic.

cancer, but why wait until you do to do what's healthy?

Shop at local Farmer's Markets whenever possible. Find out the days and times of all the local Farmer's Markets in the surrounding towns, so on any given day you have somewhere to shop if you need something. The less time you spend in supermarkets, the better. In supermarkets, confine yourself to the fruit and vegetable aisles and skip everything else. This will save time, keep you focused, and away from temptations. Don't forget your baskets or cloth bags! Watch the movie *Bag It*.

Compost food leftovers. Apartment composting systems such the All Seasons Indoor Composter and the Worm Factory Composter are now available on-line. Read *The Urban/Suburban Composter: The Complete Guide to Backyard, Balcony, and Apartment Composting* by Mark Cullen, Lorraine Johnson and Andrew Leyerle. Another option is to use a composting service if there is one in your area (they provide bins to put compost in and then do weekly curb-side pick-up). Look it up on-line and contact the nearest company: if you get enough people and/or businesses interested they may be willing to service your area.

Movies to watch: *Hungry for Change, Super Size Me, Food Matters, Fat, Sick and Nearly Dead, Fresh, Vegucated, Forks Over Knives, Farmaggedon, Food Inc.*

Home and Work

How many bags of garbage do you put out every week? Set yourself a goal, such as halving it. Watch the movie, *Garbage! The Revolution Starts at Home.*

Set up recycling bins in or near kitchens and bathrooms. Make it a family event. Watch the movie *Trashed*.

Reduce water by taking shorter showers and not letting the water run while you brush your teeth. Invest in a dual flush toilet for your home and work place.

Garden

Reduce water in your garden by zone planting and using drip irrigation.

Have your soil tested if you are growing your own vegetables: you don't want to eat your own home-grown lead-cadmium-or-chromium-laden vegetables. You can find soil testing companies on-line, just mail in a sample of your soil.

Clothing

Buy clothing made of natural materials such as organic cotton, hemp and wool. Read *Killer Clothes* by Brian and Anne Marie Clement.

Limit bra wearing and don't wear ones that restrict lymph flow. Read *Dressed to Kill: The Link Between Breast Cancer and Bras* by Sydney Singer and Soma Grismaijer, *Get It Off! Understanding the Cause of Breast Pain, Cysts and Cancer* by Sydney Singer and Soma Grismaijer.

Mind

We spend an inordinate amount of time keeping our mind entertained or busy with sound, television, news, glossy images, movies and stories in magazines. Be picky about what you hear and see. Become attuned to how much light and noise is around you; how many images pass before your eyes; how many people and distractions are around you at any one time. This will clean your system so you are neither overly emotional nor untouched by your world.

Don't allow yourself to be exposed to negative information, news, etc. Sift out anything or anyone that sensationalizes events or focuses on disasters, including people, magazines and newspapers. Look at positive influences, such as Yes! Magazine.

Practice doing one thing at a time. Most of us have become extraordinarily good at multi-tasking. The challenge is now to do one thing at a time. We tend to be vigorous with our activity choices rather than thoughtful.

Begin your day with a super-food smoothie and/or homemade green juice. The nutrients and minerals will feed your brain and keep your mind alert.

Meditate.

Challenge your way of thinking: get into interesting and inspiring conversations with people who think differently than you do. Watch *Ted Talks: Ideas Worth Spreading* at Ted.com. Listen to: *On Being* with Krista Tippett at onbeing.org; interviews on *Sounds True* at soundstrue.com; and on Spirituality and Health at spiritualityhealth.com.

Get rid of your television. Read *Remotely Controlled: How Television is Damaging our Lives* by Aric Sigman, *The Plug-In Drug: Television, Computers, and Family Life* by Marie Winn, *Four Arguments for the Elimination of Television* by Jerry Mander.

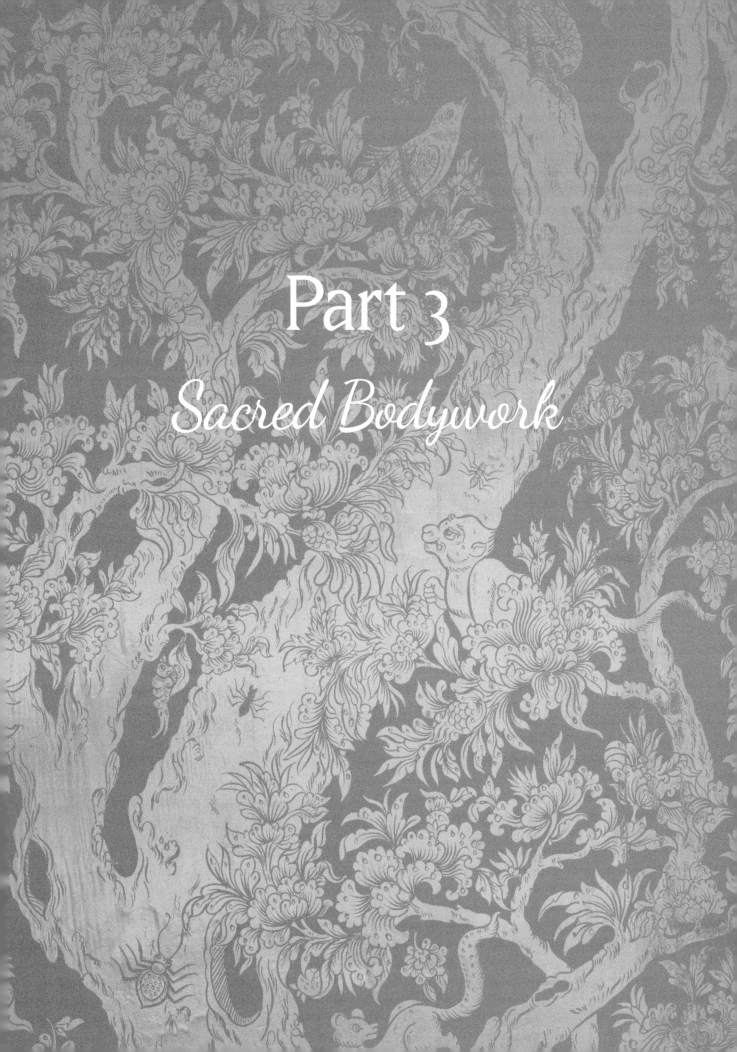

Part 3

Sacred Bodywork

Sacred Bodywork Revealed

Touching the Body, Changing our World

Research tells us that without touch, we simply cannot survive. Our hearts and souls long for, and need desperately, to be touched. In each touch, as in each soul, lives a world unspoken. As our yearning increases in this age of digital communication, more and more people turn to Massage and Bodywork Professionals to satisfy this giver-of-life.

Touch is so natural, so deeply connected to our soul that when we curl up safely in its fingers, we put aside our stories of who we are, what we do and what has happened to us. We put aside blame and protection for the experience of the here and now. At first, without our stories, blame, protection and all that we carry with us, what remains may seem small, meager compared to what was, but then as we touch our soul, we expose the root that connects all.

Rather than our bodies being a possession we *own*, as in 'my body,' and rather than living *in* our bodies, we experience ourselves as a complete organism. And rather than living *in* this world, we are of one breath, bound together, again, a complete organism. Organisms only survive within a specific set of circumstances—we cannot cut it, scar it, use toxic chemicals on it, blow it (or each other) up without traumatizing and jeopardizing the organism as a whole.

It is time to care for and heal this body, this world of ours, this organism, and it is by actively nurturing a deep and real connection to it and to ourselves, that we change both ourselves and the world.

It begins with Touch, the profound sea. Not the surface hand on skin, and not the blunt force of an elbow, but with connection, a contact that allows us to go deep, to plunge in to our Earth, to fly out into our Heaven and to connect the two.

Healing the Energetic Matrix

It is known that massage and bodywork is good for the *body*, that it can alleviate physical stress and tension, decrease physical discomforts, aches and pains. Many massage professionals use it to enhance athletic performance, to facilitate healing after surgery or illness, and towards a multitude of other goals.

However, massage is also a powerful force of healing for the other aspects that make up the totality of the complicated and multi-dimensional beings we are: the energetic matrix.

The energetic matrix is made up of not only our physical body (Earth), but our emotional, spiritual, dream and energetic bodies (Heaven). It is within this matrix that we may store our life experiences, thoughts, memories, emotional and behavioral patterns, as well as the holding patterns of the physical body.

Storing creates blockages, distortions or disruptions in our matrix, and in the more subtle levels of the energetic matrix; the flows and patterns of energy such as chakras and meridians.

A Dual Path encompasses two approaches: Sacred Practices and Sacred Bodywork and uses these paths to explore both what we store in our energetic matrix *and* how distortions and blockages in our matrix have affected us. It then clears and shifts our energetic matrix so we can move forward into an awakened sense of ourselves.

Heavenly Elevator

The magical and otherworldly experiences of Sacred Bodywork put us in direct contact with spirit, temporarily and sometimes permanently liberating us from our burdens. These direct experiences are easily overlooked for what they are: a new reference point, a new set point for our operating system.

Sacred Bodywork, by allowing for this meeting with our spirit, becomes the great connector between the infinite potential of Heaven (through spontaneous dissociation from self, out of body experiences, etc.) and the Earth patterns and limitations that solidify in our physical body. It is the elevator that takes us directly to another world. Whether the elevator doors close really fast and we just catch a glimpse or we step right through the doors to whatever awaits us on the other side, these often overlooked experiences serve as place markers for Heaven. The more familiar we are with where Heaven can be found within, the easier it is to find our way there.

The Dual Path is designed to change your fundamental core being. If you do not like what you see within and around you, know this is often a natural part of the process. Allow yourself to drift through and over this rocky ocean with patience and a gentleness, opening to what and who emerges on the other side.

Keep in mind this is a *process* of change and transformation. As they say, life is a journey, not a destination.

The Meaning of Deep Work

When a client asks for deep work they are asking the therapist to press deeply into the tissue, often using forearms and elbows, and sometimes knees or feet. The client who requests deep work has made a predetermination of what they want or need, and often has no sense if their body, or a part of their body such as the glutes, stomach or shoulders, has an adverse reaction to the work such as clenching as the pressure is applied.

A Sacred Bodyworker has different goals, and rather than using a predetermined technique, will choose the *right* technique to achieve their goal. Sacred Bodywork involves listening for information and working with the subtleties of the body. If we press deep into the tissue solely to satisfy the client's need, we bypass most of these subtleties and end up working with the physical body alone. It is no longer a Sacred Bodywork session.

"The heart of healing lies in our ability to listen, to preceive, more than in our application of technique."

TOM MYERS,
ANATOMY TRAINS

Those who ask for deep tissue work often present with a hardened body and have been known to ask whether their hardened mass of muscle is bone. They often have areas of the body that feel closer in consistency to stone or wood than to flesh. This may come from layers of protection (physical or emotional) which then forms an impenetrable body, no matter how hard someone pushes. In Sacred Bodywork, the request for deep work is simply an expression of a yearning to be deeply touched, for someone to go beyond the barrier that has numbed them. Deep work for us *is* about going deep, but not necessarily hard into the skin and muscle. It is about listening deeply—an opportunity for the client to listen closely and deeply to themselves and an opportunity to *feel* deeply seen and listened to.

Touching the soul
is not like putting
your hand in a flame
and pulling out quickly
because it is hot.

Touching the soul
spreads like a root
encompassing
self, nature and other.

In Sacred Bodywork, the need or desire for deep work tells us the client is in some way Earth-bound, that there is a density to their energy, and that their way of thinking, habits and patterns most likely reflect this density. The denser the energy, the deeper the grooves in the mind, and the more repetitious the patterns. Dense energy expresses itself by keeping things in place. In physical terms, the muscles recognize the length they should be; the shoulders are held at a particular height; and tightness and tension are repeatedly found in the same areas of the body. As we 'de-densify' the energy through Sacred Bodywork, the mind lets go of the matrix it has created and collapses into a new, healthier one closer to its original energetic blueprint.

These clients often respond exceedingly well if we begin with a firm touch and deep work and transition to more subtle work. It is these clients who are likely to have kriyas since so much of their energy is bound up.

Bridging the Gap between the Physical and Subtle Bodies

Some Massage and Bodywork Professionals such as those who do Rolfing, Structural Integration, Deep Tissue, Sports Massage, those dedicated to injuries, work primarily with the physical body: skin, muscle, fascia and structure. At the other end of the spectrum are bodyworkers who may not even touch the body at all, but work with energy or chi, sound and vibration or crystals. Sandwiched in-between these two ends of the spectrum are a host of other modalities, including Swedish Massage, Thai Massage, Tui Na, Acupressure, Reflexology, Lymphatic Massage and Shiatsu.

Professionals on the former end of this spectrum are often attracted there by their interest in the physical body, a drive to know the facts and a belief that the physical realm is the only one that is 'real' or that they have an interest in. Considering this approach from a business perspective, it is considered to carry the least amount of risk.

Those on the latter end of the spectrum often have a sense, or belief, that there is more to us than flesh and bone. It often attracts those with a *natural ability*, such as intuition, a strong draw to the magic, the unknown, the inexplicable, the mysteries of the body. From a business perspective, this approach is considered to carry the highest amount of risk, and coincidentally tends to draw those who lack business skills, those who do the work because of a gravitational pull that has nothing to do with marketing or finances.

These two ends of the spectrum can represent very different creatures, known to sniff each other with disdain, believing the other is doing nothing of value.

The profoundest changes come through the subtlest of touch.

But the truth of it is that all of us are of great value to those who are responsive to our particular craft.

Sacred Bodywork allows us to honor ourselves in our entirety and for many clients and professionals, Sacred Bodywork is the perfect bridge: we are no longer obligated to choose one aspect over another and we no longer have to separate the spirit from the body. We can finally embrace both our humanness and our sacredness.

The Dual Path has a toe in each
pond and draws from both wells,
addressing connections between physical
pain, emotional or energetic imbalances and
blockages, tension, and spiritual dis-ease.
The Dual Path rebuilds the broken bridge
that has for too long divided us
allowing us to walk through a door,
a door that opens into a world with
potentially no end,
no barriers,
as deep and wide as the universe itself,
into a world that transforms us all.
When we open to our experience,
lifting the limited veil of education,
the mysteries of the body lets us know
we are standing on sacred ground.
Only then can we honor the whole
of the spectrum,
and ourselves in our entirety.

Energy (moves) from higher vibrational energies into denser form.

Finally, the energy becomes so dense that it 'condenses' into physical form.

The energy goes from Primal neutral source (Tao), Realms of pure spirit, Causal realms (unemotional mind), Astral realms (thoughts take on qualities of subtle emotional charge) to Physical realm.

An understanding of this configuration is crucial in understanding the patterns of health and disease.

Currents of thought and emotion mold the physical body...

FRANKLYN SILLS
THE POLARITY PROCESS

To Heaven, via Earth

Sacred Bodywork is itself a Dual Path, working with Earth, the physical body, to access Heaven, the sacred.

Numerous systems of belief say not only are we more than our flesh and our thoughts, but that we are various planes of being that culminate in the physical body. Over time, many names have evolved for the various aspects that make up the totality of who we are and there has been much discussion over each of their definitions:

The Physical Body	The Subtle Body
The Mental Body	The Divine Body (Tantrism)
The Emotional Body	The Light or the Rainbow Body
The Dream Body	(Tibetan Buddhism)
The Causal Body	The Body of Bliss (Kriya Yoga)
The Astral Body	The Immortal Body (Hermeticism)
The Etheric	The Diamond Body (Taoism)
The Spiritual Body	The Supracelestial Body (Sufism)

The Mental Body is made of thought, just as the Emotional Body consists of emotions and the Physical Body is made of matter. Some say the spirit, causal and light bodies are one and the same, that each body has a different density, vibrates at its own specific frequency and corresponds to a particular plane of existence.

Then there are energetic patterns that describe particular flows or patterns of energy in our system:

- The chakra system or soul centers
- The meridian system
- Kundalini energy
- Auras
- Longline currents
- Transverse currents
- Spiral currents
- Positive, negative and neutral

At the moment of conception our energetic matrix, or blueprint, is undistorted and untainted; we are energetically clear. However, humans are complicated, fragile, sensitive and multi-dimensional creatures and everything we experience from that moment on has an effect on this matrix.

If our parents are stressed, fight and yell while we are in utero, this effects our energetic matrix. Siblings who resent or are jealous of us, friends who betray us, a car accident, a teacher who takes a dislike to us, anything and everything has an effect on our energetic matrix.

Imagine a jigsaw puzzle, nicely put together on a table top. This represents the stability, strength and health of our energetic matrix at conception. Now visualize a hand or finger coming from underneath and pushing up, and the distortions this creates in the pieces as slight disconnections and spaces form and they angle away from each other. It is no longer one puzzle, but a bunch of pieces trying to cling on to each other.

In *our* systems, disruptions and distortions in our energetic matrix are expressed in our behavior, habits, emotions, stresses and the way we hold our bodies. These disruptions quickly form patterns which can be difficult to change.

Sacred Bodywork uses the physical body (earth) as an access point to a deeper level of connection that affects not only the physical body, but *all* our bodies and all our patterns: our entire energetic matrix.

This is the Dual Path, working with the physical body, Earth, to facilitate the client's access to Heaven. Alone, these experiences and otherworldly journey's are powerful and wonderful, but it is in combination with the Sacred Practices that they make their real contribution.

The Dual Path of Client and Professional

Both the client and the professional are on the Dual Path, receiving Sacred Bodywork and working with the Sacred Practices, each moving towards actively clearing their energetic matrix, both within the session, and outside the session.

The world of the client and that of the professional are parallel journeys of exploration, discovery, contemplation, opening and transformation.

One of my very first clients came to me because she was a teacher of small children. Every day she sat on their small chairs, chairs not made for her adult body. She complained of continual back and neck discomfort and pain. I focused my work on these areas in the hope of relieving her discomfort. She continued to return every week. After some time, it dawned on her that prior to commencing these weekly sessions she had caught every sniffle and sickness the children had come to school with, but now she couldn't remember the last time she'd been sick!

There's nothing like personal experience. We can read all the research on how Massage and Bodywork strengthens the immune system, but once we have experiences like this, it's simple, we *know*. Together, the client and professional discover a truth. The client benefits from the outcome of this magic and takes this truth into their world, maybe recounting their experience in a conversation here and there, while the professional sits with the magic of their profession each and every day.

Another client, also one of my first, started to have headaches at the end of her sessions. She would have wonderfully relaxing sessions but leave with a headache. I was concerned I was doing something wrong and that was inadvertently causing her headaches, and my discomfort at this prospect drove me to look for something that I could do to remedy the situation. In my research, I came across something called "fluffing the aura". It sounded hokey but there were directions, and, without telling her, I followed them, slowly and gently waving my hands around her head. She left without a headache. The next session I didn't 'fluff' —headache. The next session I fluffed; no headache. I hardly knew what I was doing and certainly didn't believe in it, but here I was "fluffing auras" and finding it effective.

Drums, crystals, feathers, dream, spirit, emotional or psychological bodies… are not that much further down the path from the starting point of working with the physical body.

A client once asked,
"I've been to see many bodyworkers,
and many of them,
like you,
have rooms peppered with unusual things.
Some of you have crystals, Buddhas, drums, feathers.
Are you all special people, born with these interests or knowledge,
or did you become that way over time?"
It was a fabulous question and one
I'd never been asked before.
Bodyworkers are exposed to the inexplicable.
You can call them magical or strange or impossible
but the longer we are in this profession
the more of these inexplicables we are exposed to.
It can take many shapes and forms
but slowly it opens the mind,
allows us to see,
to believe,
to know,
that there are things we do not have
the answers to.
Sometimes it allows us the honor
or recognize a wrong turn,
a path not taken.
Sometimes it gives us the clarity to
voice our insights,
sometimes it gives us the courage to listen.

Sacred Bodywork Defined

Sacred Bodywork views the physical body as a vehicle to access spirit, or Heaven. Although it may integrate Fine Tissue work (working therapeutically on areas of pain and tightness), it does so solely to release, diffuse and dissolve *energy* that is held there and experienced as tightness, pain or discomfort. Sacred Bodywork is based on creating an extraordinarily deep level of relaxation called Systemic Relaxation that allows the mind to release its hold on us so that our body releases its holding patterns, allowing for deep shifts in our physical, spiritual and energetic body to occur. These releases and shifts, that can be deep *and* subtle, allow us to connect with our infinite potential, a much larger universe than the body we inhabit (along with its habits, behavior and emotions). Examples of these releases and shifts are listed in the World of Sacred Possibilities.

Once the client reconnects to a more infinite experience of themselves, free of anxiety or plans, floating or flying, the lighter being that is their true essence and nature, quiet time is of great importance. After the session they must spend time alone in quiet contemplation of the shifts they have experienced and to allow for absorption of energetic diffusion and refinements. This dedicated time honors what has been touched, the sacredness of our deeper self, that would otherwise be lost if we move on to the next thing on our to-do list.

Whether you stepped into the session feeling and experiencing yourself in one way and walked out in a different place within yourself, or you experienced a complete shift in consciousness, this time alone allows for absorption, acceptance and understanding. You and your experience are not separate and if we allow them to, our experiences shape us. We are often shaped by the difficulties and challenges of our lives, becoming determined, driven, hardened, protected, strong, forceful, powerful, weak, immovable, unstable, etc. To remold the shape we have become, we need to actively and deeply inhale our spirit and soul when we touch upon it.

However, if our goal is to dissolve and transform the hardened core we have become, we cannot accomplish this solely by soaking up an experience in our Sacred Bodywork session.

We *must* also work actively to deconstruct the walls and foundation of who we are. This is where the Sacred Practices come into play as they guide us further and deeper on our path of letting go of who we know ourselves to be, and assists in the full transformation into our true essence and nature.

The Dual Path Professional

Working with the physical body is to work with Earth, and the energetic body, with Heaven. In Sacred Bodywork, we touch and work with the physical body in order to access the spirit body and transport the client to heaven. While this paradigm requires releasing prescribed *systems* you may be using, it integrates and incorporates seamlessly with most bodywork techniques.

Sacred Bodywork begins with noticing and gathering information, whether it is presented verbally or otherwise, prior to or during the session. For example, someone who presents with physical issues are informing us that in addition to possible pain, discomfort, emotional or psychological trauma, their system will have energetic disruptions, stagnation or blockage. This noticing and gathering of information is ongoing throughout the session and is not a formal intake or series of tests—much of it is gathered through a bioenergetic connection which informs us of the nature of, and obstructions in, the client's tissue and energetic system. The knowledge we gather directs our goals and the particular path we take to achieve these goals.

The sessions are not filled with robust activity, or of *trying* or working hard for either the client or the therapist. Sacred Bodyworkers are relaxed and focused, connecting to the client by connecting to the moment. Letting go of everything that is not the moment creates a profound disintegration of energetic membrane between client and therapist, allowing for a deep sense of presence and connection to heart, breath, compassion, gentleness, stillness, silence and care. In essence, the professional *guides* or *leads* the client into a place that is quiet and meditative with an easy, wandering sense of direction, listening with their hands, heart and instincts, keeping their mind well out of the way.

For the professional to recognize restlessness, shades of emotion or a mind that is busy, they must have a degree of familiarity with these states as well as the path that leads to inner peace and calm. This familiarity is won and honed by being the recipient of bodywork, personal and client observation, and self-exploration through the Sacred Practices.

For the professional to lead the client to a meditative state, they must be able to access their own meditative state. Even though the client and professional are linked, going arm-in-arm through this process, the professional is the *guide** for the client. In order to effectively and ethically guide a client in matters of the body, mind and spirit, the professional *must* be on their own journey of understanding and discovery.

The Dual Path both requires and provides the opportunity for the professional to enter a learning process that moves them towards intimate knowledge of their body, mind and spirit *and* to develop a recognition of their clients. That is to say; being a Sacred Bodyworker is no less an active role and path for the professional as it is for the client.

Sacred Guides

Touch is one of the oldest, most natural and powerful means of transportation between Earth and Heaven. When our hands touch another, there is a natural joining of Heaven and Earth. Our hands, being made of matter, belong to the domain of Earth. These Earth hands of ours touch Earth bodies of skin and muscle, and in so doing create an *experience* that moves the soul and spirit, into the province of Heaven. Touch has been employed in this fashion throughout time by healers and shamans.

Today's urban healers and shamans are Massage and Bodywork Professionals, and while many clients still come to us for an Earth experience, wanting and needing their muscles to be worked, believing this is the given format to relieve their physical aches and pains, there are more and more who seek out a Heavenly route to their imbalances: a cellular, energetic, vibrational balance, clearing and reorganization.

Sacred Bodywork addresses both our physical and subtle bodies.

There are innumerable accounts of clients slipping into the realm of Heaven, connecting to the subtle body, even without effort by either the professional or the client: sensations of floating, flying and swimming, unaccounted for movement in or around the body, of images, colors and dreams that lead to an awakening, a lightness of being, a sense of openness, letting go or complete transformation.

While touch is inherently a natural transportation system between Earth and Heaven, Sacred Bodyworkers are active guides in this journey.

Note: Although our goal is to *lead* the client, they will only go as far as they are ready to. Any number of issues may block them, including fear, resistance, alertness, anticipation, inability to let go. Know that each session builds a bridge to their next step.

Guide as noted in Wikipedia: A guide is a person who leads anyone through unknown or unmapped country. This includes a guide of the real world (such as someone who conducts travelers and tourists through a place of interest), as well as a person who leads someone to more abstract places (such as to knowledge or wisdom).

Learn to sit still, to wait until your dust has settled, and your air has become clear. Wait for deep stillness. Then, start.

Above all, go slowly.

Develop intuitive perception and understanding of everything. Pay attention to everything, especially the little things. Changing the little things often brings about the largest improvements.

Treat everyone, and every part of everyone, as equal. Every cell in the body has consciousness. Every minute structure of the dreambody is a hologram.

Presence is much more important than technique. Beginners want to learn more and more techniques. When you achieve mastery, one technique will do.

It is amazing how much how little will do.

You cannot go too deep, just too fast.

Meditate, live purely, be quiet, and do your work with mastery.

Do your work, then stand back.

HUGH MILNE,
THE HEART OF LISTENING, MOTIFS

The Wonders of Heaven

Most of us want our bodies to look good, function well and be in a sound state of overall health and these tenets are often the ones that bring a client to a bodywork session. So when a client slips below the surface, through the door leading to matters of the soul and the spirit, they are as surprised as Alice falling down the rabbit hole and oftentimes on an equal journey of discovery and transformation.

As a rule, clients who specifically seek out these experiences turn to the more ethereal modalities of Reiki, Polarity, Craniosacral and, occasionally, to massage professionals. The experiences themselves are elusive, hit-or-miss and for the most part byproducts, not a *goal* or even the focus of the professional's training.

Sacred Bodywork, while promoting a sense of ease and openness rather than single-mindedness towards an expectation by either the client or the professional, sets up the *conditions* to actively encourage the opening of the doorway.

These experiences serve as a reminder that we are more than flesh and blood, more than Earth: we are also Heaven embodied. When we come home to the potency of this realization and are refining and clearing our energies through the Practices, we begin to transform our daily lives, the trajectory of our lives and our very natures.

Let go of your biology and become the totality of vibrancy.

There is no doubt that the invisible wires that spark our bodily machine can also reignite our health and revive humanity.

DRS. BRIAN AND ANNA MARIA CLEMENT
FOUNDERS OF HIPPOCRATES
HEALTH INSTITUTE
HEALING OUR WORLD,
VOLUME 31, ISSUE 4

The World of Sacred Possibilities

Do It for the Gods

He says,
"Most people graduate
from
massage
school
and start up shop
like they're setting up
a barber shop,"
He gives me a wide grin,
"but you guys,
you do massage likes it's a religion,
like you're doing it for the gods!"
Do it for the gods...

This,
my life,
is my soul,
all of it.
We must not fear to declare this, nor must
we be coy or abashed.
Know your contribution, your life,
you, can be great.
We can all be great.
We can be and remain inspired,
loving who we are.
Those of us who take this road must
develop true strength of character,
softness and flexibility,
dedication to self knowledge and growth,
a developed sense of personal ethics
and the pursuit of real health and happiness
as well as hearts that can care
without being shielded, without being punctured.
*Are you ready to strike the gong,
and welcome the gods?*

I do not believe, nor do I make the assertion, that the list I have created is complete. It is only an attempt at creating such a list. In addition, there are categories that I have chosen not to focus on, that are nonetheless experienced, such as:

- Past-life experiences, where the client feels they have lived another life. Often this experience explains a certain character or psychological dynamic or even a physical marking on their body.

- Back-to-the-seed or rebirthing, where the client re-experiences their own birth.

- Creature or animal, where the client *becomes* another creature, such as a bear or lion. This is sometimes a past-life experience.

I have not included these experiences because although they may occur in a Sacred Bodywork session, we do not specifically guide the client towards them nor are they the *goal* of the session.

In the pages that follow you will find a collection of statements by various bodywork recipients describing their experiences with the World of Sacred Possibilities:

- **Spacial Experiences: Floating, Flying, Elevation, Out-of-Body, Loss of Orientation**
- **Ghost Hands**
- **Dream-like States**
- **A Spontaneous Release of Energy (kriya), Pain or Emotion**
- **Sense of Timelessness**
- **Visual Experiences: Colors and Images**
- **Shift in Mindset**
- **Connection, to Self, Spirit or Universal**

Names in the following descriptions have been changed as requested. You are invited to add descriptions of your own experiences by going to my website.

Spacial Experiences: Floating, Flying, Elevation, Out of Body, Loss of Orientation

"I have had experiences where I feel like I am flying. I am either guided by my breath or by the soft music playing in the background during the session. I find myself in the form of a bird either floating in the wind over large canyon mountain ranges, or over soft bamboo type trees." — Stephanie

"I've had experiences of floating, of being outside my body and watching my body while it was being worked on the table, being separate and questioning, 'Wait a minute, if that's my body I'm watching, then what am I?'" — Adler

"I felt a sense of lightness and floating above the table. I've also gotten off the table and felt my feet weren't quite touching the ground and that I was gliding or floating above it in a very good way, in a way that made me feel peaceful and lighter. I think that's a nice benefit, that you feel something has unburdened you, that your muscles have released what they've been holding psychologically." — Rebecca

"I lost the sense of which direction my body was in, in relationship to the walls of the room. This was sometimes accompanied by a kind of weightlessness, a sense of "floating" in space. Quite delightful." — Lee

Ghost Hands

"I have experienced the feeling of being touched when not actually being touched. Sometimes it is the feeling that the hand is still in place even though it is no longer there... as if the energy and intent has been left in place to continue to be absorbed." — Susan

"The practitioner was working on my head and it felt like there was someone else at my feet." — Patricia

"One time I thought you were on my face and you hit a gong and you were all the way at the other end of the room! So you weren't even touching me when I thought you were touching me! At other times I would have sold my eye-tooth and said, "her hand is on my forehead," but no, it was on my toe." — Leslie

"I often feel the sensation of many hands when I know there are only two." — Anne

"I've experienced the sensation of another presence in the room, most often at my feet." — Darra

Dream-like States

"At times I feel somewhere between awake and asleep; my mind goes into a dreamlike state where I do not think in words but in colors and sounds. It's like my body transcends my mind." — Diana

"There are occasions when I have an intense sense of euphoria for hours after the session. I can sense that it will occur when I am in a semi-dream state for most of the session, which usually is initiated by me being able to watch the massage from afar initially (i.e. as a third person), and then I enter into this state of timelessness." — Bob

"The relaxation response I experience can make me feel like I'm in a waking sleep. I totally forget that I'm in the room." — Anne

Spontaneous Release of Energy (kriya), Pain, or Emotion

"I sometimes experience a spontaneous release of energy, pain or emotion that sometimes totally comes out of nowhere and is very intense, or sometimes it builds up slowly during a session and is a soft wave of release, like having warm bath water flowing out of the tub as it's being drained." — Darra

"I have had spontaneous releases. I'm not sure what kind of release it was, or if it even needs to be identified, but it certainly made me cry. The experience was so moving and beautiful. Sometimes I want to fight it, but I am reminded to let the experience fill me and then to let it go." — Stephanie

"I have had numerous experiences with kriya's at different times in my life. The most recent one I recall clearly—I was on the table and the practitioner was doing massage with polarity therapy. My whole body had a jolt of energy around my kidneys. I knew what it was but she had never experienced anything like that before so I explained it to her." — Patricia

"I have experienced kriya's in a session. For me, it starts feeling like a hot, itchy tickle at the site that is being worked on, then sort of like an explosion of energy, like a sneeze or a sigh. Afterwards, I feel much better, energized and relaxed at the same time." — Diana.

"I had a therapist working on my leg when it twitched rather violently. After that, problems I had been having with my knee and walking completely disappeared. I still feel like this was quite an amazing experience. It was a huge release." — MSR

"I experience kriya's several times during my massages. It usually happens after pain points have been removed and I can literally feel the energy flow released in my body. It is a wonderful feeling." — Anonymous

"I've experienced many releases of energy where I felt the release of stress or pressure through pressure pointing and other massage techniques. The rush for me is usually a deep breath and release of air, or a twitch, or sense of relief." — Roberta

"I've had kriya's at least a dozen times. I would describe it as a whole body spasm, where my body seems to jump, combined with a short quick breath and a rush of energy." — Deanna.

Sense of Timelessness

"A really good massage will bring me into my center, to a place of deep peace and stillness. During this time, it can also feel like time is suspended and all is well. Depending on the massage, how willing I am to surrender to this stillness, the skills of the practitioner and what else is going on during that day determines how long I stay in this feeling of timelessness. It can be for the entire massage, a few hours afterwards or even longer." — Karen

"Unless the session has more of a physical focus, there is almost always a sense of timelessness if the practitioner is good and I can trust to let go." — Anita

"The time distortion that occurs is one hallmark of a hypnotic state, and allows me to feel both calmer and more refreshed afterward." — Judith

"There is no concept of time during a session for me—it passes either very quickly or very slowly." — Fiona

Visual Experiences: Colors and Images

"During a massage, when deeply relaxed, I experience meditative and hypnotic states—sometimes seeing colors, sometimes experiencing a sense of floating in water while watching beautifully colored coral, sea anemones and tropical fish. Often I feel my muscles kinesthetically "melt," give up, or even change color as they let go." — Judith

"I see colors and images a lot and often see old, sepia-toned faces that look like they're photographs swirling across my eyes from left to right, just blurry enough that I can't make out the faces or recognize anyone--they seem very old. I also see colors, lights, pulses, feel heat, cold, etc." — Darra

"I experience colors with practitioners who seem to be connected, grounded and present. I see colors which are in varying shapes and often morph shape during the session.

It is a most precious energy. I don't know if it is the practitioner leading or my state of mind leading the colors. I often get green, indigo, red, white...." — Susan

"There came a moment during the massage when I was very aware of the presence of a cat. I could see the cat near me, sitting up, looking at me in complete stillness. The only message I feel certain that the cat had for me was: "I am here." I don't know how long the cat was with me, but I was aware when it no longer was. At that moment, I asked if there was a cat in the room, for the cat's presence seemed too real for it not to have been. I was told there was not. I didn't have a cat at the time, I don't have a cat now, and have always considered myself more of a dog person. So it was surprising to have my "visitor" come in this form! No, not just a visitor—more than that, my cat was a gift." — Peggy

Shift in Mindset

"I've experienced a 'shift' in mindset often as powerful as walking into a session feeling distressed and leaving feeling euphoric! Amazing how powerful a session can be! It's facilitated by a combination of ambience and energy that for me goes beyond the sense of touch: It is more of a "tuning-in" with the practitioner's guidance to allow 'tuning out' from whatever I brought to the session. I don't always remember the details but I know that afterwards something has shifted." — Fiona

"I have experienced a lovely sense of lightness, like all my concerns and worries have been erased. I often feel much more present in my body and soul." — Darra

"There have been many sessions where I've entered a different space in my mind and my body, where I've felt a sense of calm, of peace and serenity. I often feel euphoric, relaxed and at peace and able to go with the flow." — Elie

"Massage sessions almost always bring me to a calm state of being instead of my usual, and sometimes frantic, state of doing and anticipating, worrying about the future. That's a pretty amazing transformation in an hour's worth of massage." — Kalo

"I feel like I am more in my body and also outside of myself in some transcendent way that brings perspective to issues that may have otherwise seemed unapproachable. I feel better both physically and mentally, and am able to see some of the choices I need to make in a better light." — Diana

Connection, to Self, Spirit, or Universe

"There is an intangible sense that I am more connected with myself and the world as a whole. I feel all around more in tune with everything." — Diana

"The obvious benefit is an immediate sense of connection and grounding, a reintegration that allows me to continue to feel balanced well beyond the session." — Louise

"My spirit usually feels contented and connected with my life force." — Liz

"One time, I felt my brother's spirit in the room. He was killed a few years ago in a car

accident. We were very close in age and I still feel very connected to him. He comes to me in my dreams. During the massage experience, I just felt his presence around me. When I told the massage therapist, she had felt him too. So amazing!" — Stephanie

Sacred Bodywork Premises

Sacred Bodywork premises are divided into the following categories:

- The Energetic Matrix
- A Transportation System
- Monitoring and Witnessing
- Systemic Relaxation
- Quality of Contact
- Stillness and Movement
- The Physical Body
- The Mind

The Energetic Matrix

Our energetic matrix consists of various patterns of energy that coexist while intersecting, overlapping and flowing independently of each other. It resembles a complicated, multi-patterned, three-dimensional spider web.

This web consists of our physical, energetic, spiritual and dream body as well as specific patterns of energy such as the meridian and chakra systems. Any experiences, memories and emotions can become like an insect caught in the web, creating distortions, disruptions or gaps in the original blueprint of our energetic matrix.

These are most often those things we intentionally or inadvertently hold onto, such as what we perceive as the best of times, perhaps college experiences, or the worst of times, perhaps our high school years. Army and war experiences are prime candidates for this dynamic, since they often entail forming a brother or sisterhood that is stronger or just as strong as a family bond. Trauma's, falls, accidents, being made to feel incompetent or inadequate, being shamed or violated, abusive relationships, a slap across the face or an angry voice, even a mean sibling or parent can all get stuck in the matrix. All these experiences can become our memories, they can all carry emotional content and they can all create distortions in any one, or all, of the facets of our energetic matrix; our physical, emotional, spiritual and energetic body.

A system with distortions, blockages or disruptions causes a host of complications that may include fatigue, depressed immune systems, illness, compensational and unhealthy behaviors including our relationship to self-image. In response we often pursue coping mechanisms, the most common being an unhealthy use of alcohol, tobacco, drugs, pornography, food and relationships, and an immersion in television, gaming, gambling, texting and the internet.

Sadly we are at a point where for many the difference between what is healthy and unhealthy is blurred, not because we are confused but because many of our coping mechanisms bring us pleasure or an escape and is therefore challenging or unpleasant to imagine a life without them. If you think of what it would be like for you to give up coffee, ice-cream, pasta or cheese, that's just skimming the surface of what, for many, it's like to give up deep-seated coping mechanisms.

On the other hand we may seem quite healthy and not recognize that even though we don't have unhealthy coping mechanisms, *we still live with the damage* of these distortions and blockages. The *damage* is often an unwelcome burden or may even be sanctioned as part of our personal identity and character in the form of:

- unhealthy emotional and behavioral patterns
- negative emotions such as anger, frustration, irritation, impatience, depression
- an inability to truly and deeply relax
- always ready to do something, be on the go, not in the moment
- difficulty sleeping, nightmares, a busy mind, controlling, Type A personality
- generalized anxiety, tension or worry
- discomfort or pain
- spaceyness, confusion, feeling lost
- a loss of, or disconnection from, the self

While these manifestations of internal energetic disruption impede our everyday functioning, they also impede our connection to self, other, soul and spirit.

The Sacred Bodywork Professional allows energetic impediments to inform and orchestrate their work: to dissipate,

The energy goes from Primal neutral source (Tao), Realms of pure spirit, Causal realms (unemotional mind), Astral realms (thoughts take on qualities of subtle emotional charge) to Physical realm. An understanding of this configuration is crucial in understanding the patterns of health and disease...

Energy moves from higher vibrational energies into denser form. Finally, the energy becomes so dense that it 'condenses' into physical form. Currents of thought and emotion mold the physical body...

FRANKLYN SILLS
THE POLARITY PROCESS

refine and transmute these disruptions and blockages, ferrying the client to finer and subtler realms.

The dissipation and transmutation of this energy, whether through the charged passage of a kriya or gentle melting, is not only vital to all aspects of our health: physical, emotional, behavioral, psychological and spiritual but *is what allows the spirit to awaken.*

A Transportation System

The techniques that follow were developed or chosen because of their capacity to ferry the client to other realms. However the professional cannot be a competent guide without a personal familiarity with their own holding patterns, meditative states and experience with dropping into their own dream or spirit body.

This personal experience allows us, with practice, to identify and monitor the client's state of mind and body. There must be ample practice of not only the physical techniques but also monitoring the stages of decreasing physical and mental holding, and the increase and deepening of breath and release in our client.

Once this stage of our learning has been accomplished, we can become the guide and *lead* our client onto this transportation system from Earth to Heaven.

Monitoring and Witnessing

We receive information through words, facial expressions, tone of voice, changes in breathing rates, and what we feel, sense and intuit. There are five opportunities to witness and monitor what is being expressed or held in a client's energetic matrix:

- During phone or other contact prior to the session
- On arrival for their session (including frustration with the intake process, traffic and parking)
- Observations made when they are on the table (such as fidgeting, talking,)
- When we lay our hands near or on them
- Once the session is over (including rushing off to their next appointment, immediately getting on the phone)

Sacred Bodywork is slow and meditative, and in this state of consciousness the professional can be sensitive and available to the stream of information that flows within and around the client. Monitoring this constant influx of information through all of our senses is built into the techniques and the sensibility with which we do our work.

What we notice, or monitor, are such things as changes in depth, rate and patterns of breath and whether these changes are associated with pain and the physical body, with the emotional body and/or a deepening level of relaxation. We monitor releases in a muscle or a limb and the changes the release brings, as well as movement within the system as a whole, and individual parts of the body.

As gentle and compassionate witnesses, we simply honor and are present with whatever is in the client's energetic field. Monitoring, or being witness to these subtle shifts honors the deepest and most hidden aspects of our client. This rare procedure has a deeply calming effect on their entire system.

Systemic Relaxation

Systemic Relaxation is the *result* and *manifestation* of honoring, monitoring and addressing the system and the energetic matrix as a whole rather than the body alone.

Systemic Relaxation is a deep and complete state of relaxation which goes beyond the everyday level of 'relaxation', and affects the entire *system*, including body chemistry, brain and thought function and muscular skeletal holding patterns.

The client often then slips with ease from this state into their dream and spirit body, circumventing the physical and emotional body and having an otherworldly influence on their sense of time, space and self.

Quality of Contact

The *quality* of contact and connection is sustained, warm, and calm. Every part of the therapist's body that makes contact—hand, fingers, arms or elbows, is used to connect with the underlying currents and to receive information, rather than to apply pressure (although a good deal of pressure may be applied, the goal and focus remains the same). All parts of the hand—the palm, both eminences and the fingers—must develop sensitivity, responsiveness and the ability to detect, map and stay in contact with the client's internal terrain and innate movement within the client's body. Stiff hands and fingers, even if strong, are blind and weak in their abilities. Fluid hands are perceptive and able to discover subtleties and nuances in the body's landscape.

Stillness and Movement

Stillness is extremely powerful in its ability to still the mind and deepen the breath while shifting the system into dropping in to a profound and often extended state of relaxation.

Even though Sacred Bodywork Professionals make full use of the spectrum between stillness and movement, because the foundation of Sacred Bodywork is meditative and built on monitoring and slowing the clients system, contact naturally leans towards stillness. Which point on the spectrum we use is contingent on our goal at any given moment and what we perceive of the clients energetic matrix.

For example, when a client is agitated, impatient or restless on the table, it may be best not to fight against their energy but to match it with more movement in the initial stages of the session. On the other hand, stillness in the form of a prolonged compression may work just as well to deactivate their system. Keep in mind, *stillness* does not necessarily mean a *light* touch, just one without movement over or into the body; we can be still at any depth into the body.

Stillness is also not to be mistaken for an absence of doing, or even an absence of movement (movement is from within the clients system, not ours). There is movement within stillness and it is our job to listen for it. It is this listening and sense of honoring that allows the client to feel so deeply seen and heard that in turn they can deeply relax, and let go.

The Physical Body

Areas of physical discomfort and pain need to be acknowledged with early contact and when present, is often considered a starting point for the session. Otherwise the client's mind may tell them what you are doing is not addressing their issue. However, this early contact can range from Fine Tissue Work to simply connecting to the underlying forces, enabling us to deactivate and calm both the area and the clients concerns.

Movement, repositioning and fidgeting may simply be indications of physical discomfort, which can often be easily addressed. The client's physical comfort level, which contributes greatly to the success of a Sacred Bodywork session, is covered in Part 4: The Client and Professional Guide. On the other hand, if the movement and fidgeting is reflective of irritated or overactive energy, it can be addressed by:

- Beginning the session with solid contact to ground the energy
- Matching their energy with faster initial movements, eventually slowing and deepening in focus
- Fluid whole-body strokes to dissipate the energy
- Deep compression contacts to deactivate the system
- Finding and going to the Gravitational Field

The Mind

If we are not already convinced, the fact that so many of us have trouble sleeping and meditating tells us that the mind has a tendency towards busyness. It holds ideas, worries, plans, memories, anxiety, associated emotions, hopes, dreams, disappointments and failures as if it were afraid these things will be forgotten or not dealt with (which may indeed be the truth).

Working on and around the head facilitates release so that the mind is free to wander away from what usually holds its attention. Early on in the session, we assess the degree of holding by tuning in to the level of tension, stabilization, contraction and expansion in the head and the face. We return to this area periodically during the session, including when the client is supine, to relieve any facial compression from being in the prone position and the renewed sense of awakeness and awareness that can come from being face-up.

To bring energy down from the head, and the client deeper into their system, begin the session with Spirit Welcome at the feet and make your way up the body to the head.

The professional who is familiar with how holding and releasing expresses itself in their own mind and body is more likely to be able to hone this work to the client specifically rather than doing a generalized head and face massage.

Mind Relaxing Techniques

- Clear the Confusion (Visionary Craniosacral)
- Ear Cupping (Craniosacral)
- Chakra balancing (Polarity)
- Spirit Welcome
- Golden Butterfly Opens the Window
- Melting at the head
- Massage to the muscles of the face and head

Sacred Bodywork Techniques

Sacred Bodywork techniques are not techniques we *do to the client*, they are techniques that allow us to detect and diffuse disturbances in the energetic matrix, melt through the physical body and connect with the clients entire ecosystem. The state of the professionals mind will often reflect our results, so clearing our own energetic matrix, meditating and doing the other Sacred Practices will nurture the meditative state that can help accomplish this.

I suggest exploring the following techniques by:

- Employing various levels of listening and attention
- Shifting the focus of your listening and attention
- Trying them at various depths and speeds
- Both using and omitting Melting, if Melting is integral to the technique

Exploring in this way will aid you to hone in on what contributes to its efficacy on an experiential level.

Clear the Confusion*

Sitting at the head, use your thumbs to contact glabella and slowly, firmly and gently apply pressure as you move your contact along the falx cerebri, into the hairline. If you feel the Gravitational Field of this move, stop and hold. Your contact, as with most of these techniques, should always be attuned to the nuances below the surface and allow for and facilitate expansion. Listen to your intuition to know whether to do Clear the Confusion once or to repeat it two or three times. If you repeat it, notice any differences.

1. At the start of this movement sequence, begin with contact at glabella.
2-3. Using a little oil, draw your thumbs slowly towards you.

Ear Cupping*

Sitting at the head, slowly place your hands over the ears, covering them completely. The hands are cupped rather than flat, creating a space between your hands and the ears. Hold in place, being sensitive to the breath, and any movements, energetic or otherwise.

  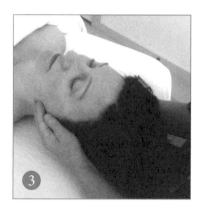

1-3. Three different views of Ear Cupping. Notice the hands are not flat, they are cupped, creating space between them and the ears.

4. Ear Cupping while the client is prone.

* These may be considered adaptations of Milne's techniques. For the original description of Hugh Milne's techniques, see *The Heart of Listening*

Chakra Balancing

All contacts in this technique use *only* the middle finger, the fire finger. Begin with the finger of the right hand at the hair line, an inch or two from the center line, and the left finger on, or around, the left tmj and hold. Left finger remains in place while the right moves to mid-point of the mandible. Hold. Right finger remains in place and left moves to mid-point on the clavicle.

This is the halfway point. Slowly withdraw contact and start the placement again, beginning with the fire finger on the left hairline, an inch or two from the center line, and the right finger on the tmj point. Right finger stays where it is, left finger moves to mandible. Left finger stays in position, right finger moves to clavicle.

Note that except when switching at the halfway point, there is always one finger that remains in contact. Placement and removal of each contact is a slow movement into their field and out again, holding for as long as you feel a magnetic pull. When you move to a new placement, it should feel as if you have been released from your contact. The precise placement, including vortex and depth of each contact, is found by tuning into the Gravitational Field.

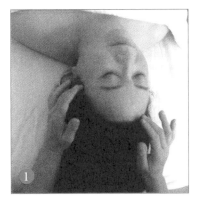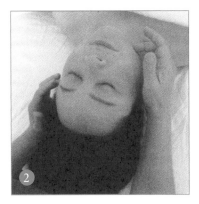

1. This sequence begins with the right finger on hairline, left on tmj. 2. Left finger on tmj, right on mandible. 3. Right finger on mandible, left on clavicle.

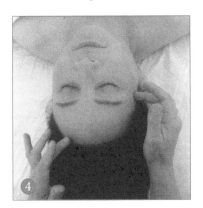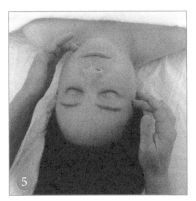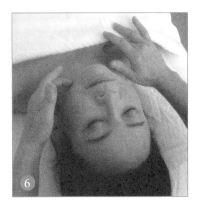

4, 5 and 6. Gently and slowly remove both contacts and repeat, beginning with left fire finger on hairline and right finger on tmj.

North/South Technique

North/South work moves energy along the longitudinal lines, up and down the body.

This can be achieved by using a technique similar to the long strokes of effleurage. In effleurage, generally, both hands move in the same direction, while in Sacred Bodywork they also move in opposite directions to each other, simultaneously moving energy from North to South and South to North. The speed of this technique varies but is often slow. It can be effectively used over joints to unblock stagnant energy that is prone to accumulate at these locations.

Longitudinal rocking is also a form of North/South work and can be done anywhere on the Stillness/Movement scale, except full Stillness. Common places of contact are at the shoulders or the feet.

North/South and East/West rocking is used for energetic and physical evaluation and to diffuse and move blockages. It also passively loosens the whole body. Keep your eye on other parts of the body and you will begin to notice differences between an ease of movement and a tight, held, contracted system.

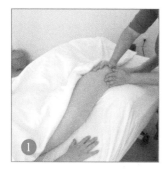   

North/South technique applied to the leg: 1. This movement sequence begins with both hands on the knee and 2 and 3. Separating towards the hip and foot and 4. Passing each other as they move towards each other again. This technique can extend all the way up the back to the shoulder and all the way down to the toes. Notice the combination of over/under as the hands move back.

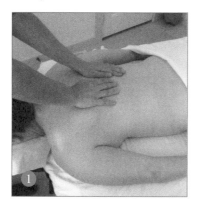 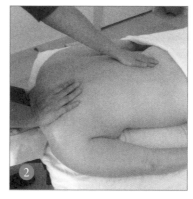

1 and 2. North/South technique applied to the back, moves slowly up and down on each side of the spine.

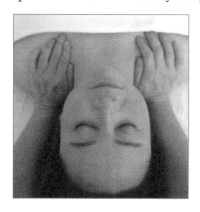 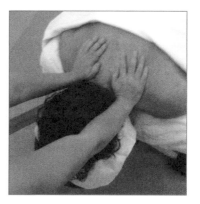

North/South technique applied to the shoulders as a rocking technique. Watch the whole body to evaluate the degree of movement and spaciousness in the body.

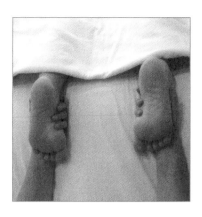
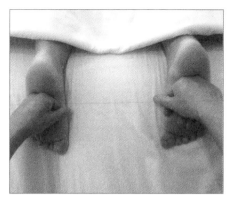

Two positions for North/South rocking applied at the feet: holding the feet or using the fists.

East/West Technique

East/West work uses the same techniques applied across (rather than up and down) a back, leg, arm or almost any part of the body. It can also be used as an assessment of East/West movement of the body or part of the body. If applied as rocking, contact may be at the feet or on the lateral edges of the legs, hips, stomach, ribs and/or shoulders. Some examples of East/West techniques:

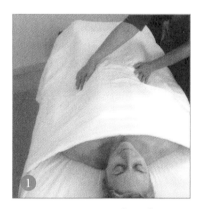
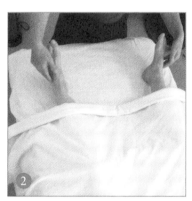

Examples of East/West technique: 1. Contact at hips as rocking. 2. Contact at the lateral side of the feet moves them medially in a rhythmic motion. 3. Sliding laterally across the back either from one side of the back to the other, or the hands can separate.

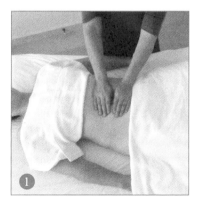
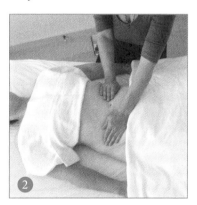
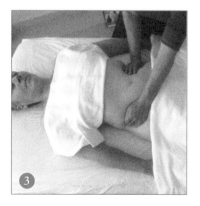

1, 2 and 3 shows the movement sequence applied to the abdomen sliding the hands across and back again. This technique can also be applied to the back.

  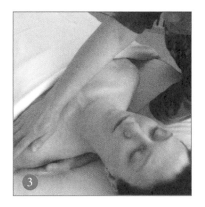

1, 2 and 3 shows East/West across the chest creating a wave–like motion as the hands slowly go back and forth.

Over and Under

Generally in a massage, the professional works with the areas of the body that are away from the table, almost never touching the surface that rests on the table. In Sacred Bodywork making contacting under the body as well as on top increases the relaxation response of the mind and body. The *Under* contact, along with Melting, is the perfect encouragement for the tissue to relax, let go, soften and sink into both the hands and the table. It is with this shift that the client may begin to lose their sense of orientation in their body.

 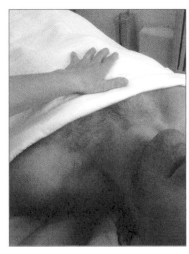 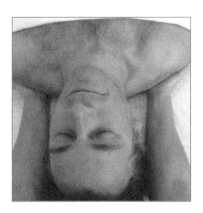

The photo in the middle shows Over / Under positions at the chest/heart chakra.

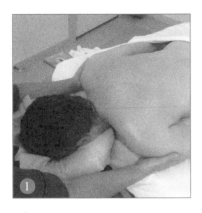

Three example of Over and Under: Photo 1 shows under contact at the shoulders, photo 2 shows an Over / Under contact at the shoulders and photo 3 shows an Over / Under contact at the shoulders with the fingertips in contact above or below the clavicle.

Spirit Welcome

Spirit Welcome follows the breath or spirit as it expands into and fills an area. It is a powerful technique to use at the soles of the feet, with thumbs making contact, on the chest with whole hand contact and at the cranium, with both hands cradling the head. This technique can begin with a firm pressure, but be sure not to compress or smother the spirit as it finds its way to you. Welcome it by acknowledging its presence and softening, creating room for it to expand further as you encourage the Melt.

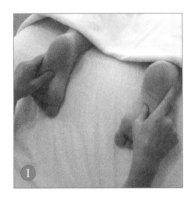
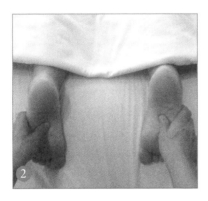
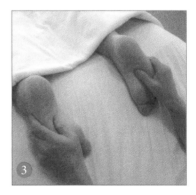

1, 2, and 3. Notice the slight difference in the angle of my hands and arms as they adjust to the angle and depth of the gravitational field.

Melting

Melting refers to a very slow release of pressure while still remaining in contact. It does not mean full disconnection. This technique allows the muscle or area that is being Melted to become aware of its holding *and* to release. The muscle or area follows the Melt, softening and letting go in tandem with the Melt. If your Melt is too fast, the area will continue holding. Note that the professional is both following the Melt and guiding the Melt. Melting can be used almost anywhere, but is particularly successful for the shoulders as an Under technique, and at the head.

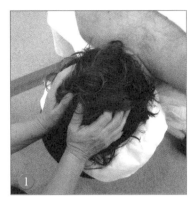 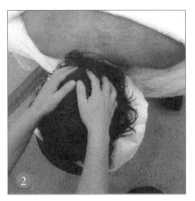

1 and 2. These photos show two different hand positions for Melting at the head while the client is prone.

 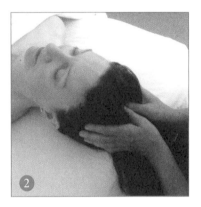

1 and 2. Melting at the head while the client is supine.

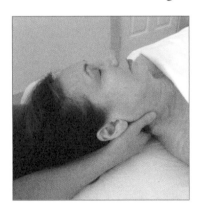 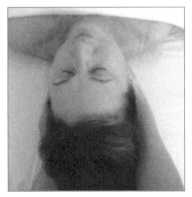 

In this example, the head is slightly tilted to the left. The right hand is on the neck and the left hand cradles the head. Both the head and neck are being Melted.

Melting Pot

On areas of energetic density (a gathering or excess of energy), Melting Pot helps release the energy, sometimes leading to kriyas (a release of energy that is visible and often expresses itself with a jolt in the body or a part of the body). These areas of energetic density are often found while Retracing Steps. The name *Melting Pot* refers to this two-handed technique, the fingers of the one hand forming a shape that is reminiscent of a pot and the thumb of second hand the spoon. The combination of the spoon applying pressure at the same time the pot diffuses pressure causes physical and/or energetic melting. Melting Pot is a technique used mostly on the back and shoulders.

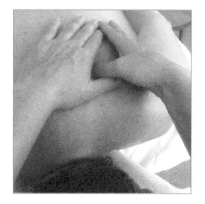 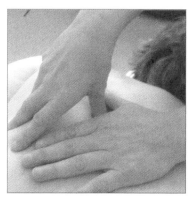 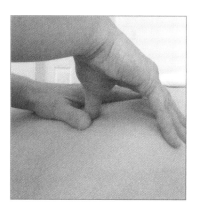

The angle of the thumb will change according to the vortex it needs to be at.

Golden Butterfly Opens the Window

Golden Butterfly Opens the Window uses Melting to relieve tension in the eyes and face. Use the thumb and middle finger to apply pressure along the eyebrow line, beginning towards the nose and moving the contacts laterally. Hold each point until there is a Melt. The name of this contact is due to the position of the hands being reminiscent of butterfly wings and the effect of this technique opening the window and having all thoughts leave.

 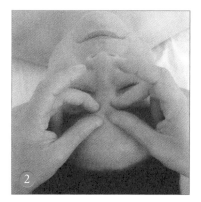 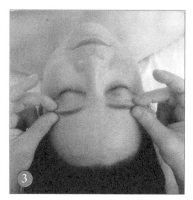

1, 2 and 3. This technique is contact that moves laterally along the eyebrow line. Pressure is applied at each contact and slowly released with a Melt.

Opening the Veil

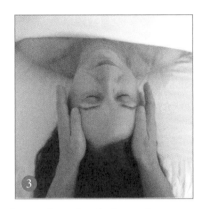

1. Opening the Veil begins at the centerline of the forehead. 2 and 3. Slowly draw the thumbs laterally. If you are called to, slowly repeat.

Softening the Clay

This technique assists the physical body in letting go, and softening. Where you feel a hardness in the body or a muscle, apply a *sustained* downward compression. Sustain this position until the compression, accompanied with the warmth of your hands (sometimes with a forearm), convinces it to let go. This is a good technique for areas that tend to hold a great deal of tension, including the hands, arms, shoulders, chest and gluteal muscles. This technique may also me combined with Melting the area, but often under the compression, softening will happen without it.

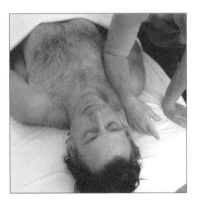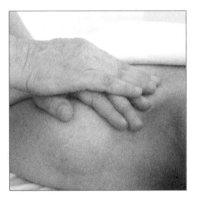

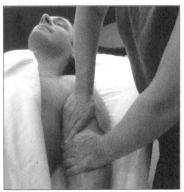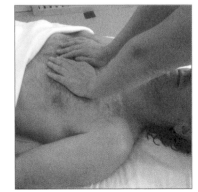

These images show Softening the Clay at various locations on the body—the shoulder, arm and chest.

Using the palm of our hand, we slowly trace an infinity sign, or the figure eight. The fullness of the back is a natural area to do this, but it can also be done on just one side of the back, across the back, the side of the torso, a leg, the stomach, chest or stomach.

1. Start at the low back, 2. Move across ,3. Up the side, 4. Towards you across the back,

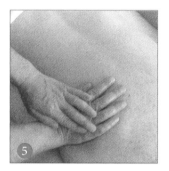 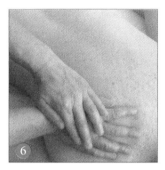 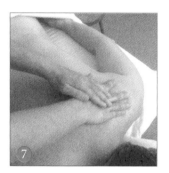 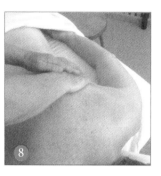

Continue up the side to the shoulder, 7. Across the top of the back, 8. Down the far side,

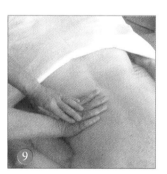 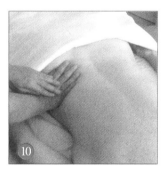 

9. Towards you as you bring your hands across the mid back, 10. To the hip and 11. Across to the starting point. Use enough oil to make the movements smooth and circular as you trace the infinity sign. Do this slowly a number of times and then reverse direction.

Riding the Waves

When the breath swells in the body, ride the wave and follow it up and out with the inhale. As the body relaxes with the exhale, ride the wave down and in. There is full and consistent contact and connection throughout: your hands and the wave are one.

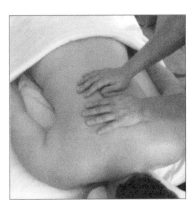

Riding the Waves calls for a sensitivity and responsiveness to the breath.

Pushing against the Wave

Applying pressure on the ribs or chest as the wave of breath begins to rise can deepen the breath.

In Pushing against the Wave, we ride the wave up and out with the inhale, and down and in again on the exhale. On the next breath, when we ride the wave in and down we stay there, applying pressure, Pushing Against the Wave, until the ribs or chest push up against our hands in almost equal amount, and then we Ride the Wave up and out again.

 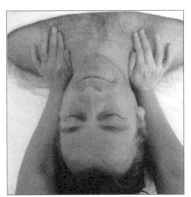 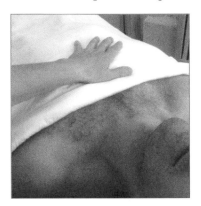

Here are 3 examples of Pushing Against the Waves. This technique can be applied with a slight restriction of the hands or with the use a lot of weight to apply the pressure. Notice that the hand positioning on the first photo could be portraying Softening the Clay, on the second, North / South Technique and the third, Riding the Waves. All three could depict Swimming with the Dolphins.

The techniques that follow are difficult to impossible to portray in photos. Some of these techniques are available in downloadable video at www.adualpath.com

Swimming with the Dolphins

Swimming with the Dolphins also begins with the breath. In Swimming with the Dolphins, as we Ride the Waves, we are simultaneously connected to breath, tissue and energy: the dolphins. We allow them to carry us along with them, in and down. We follow wherever they take us, into the deep, the unknown, the subterranean caverns and along the ridges of the reefs. We just follow, and when it's time to rise to the surface, the dolphins will carry us there.

The Gravitational Field

Rather than working everywhere and anywhere, we choose areas of the body by *looking* for areas that call to us. The *call* is the Gravitational Field; that sense that you are being magnetically pulled to an area, or that your hands are in a vortex they should not leave.

When a client informs us that they've been experiencing tight legs, headaches, sadness or stress, they are informing us of their needs, where energy may be stuck. These are the areas in their body we should feel *called to*. These areas should move us, pull us to them.

Sometimes they pull at the heart, sometimes the hands and sometimes we find our eyes drawn to an area, and drawn back again. Once there, we adjust to the depth it is drawing us to, and the vector that feels most significant.

Physical and emotional symptomatology can be used to help us hone our pull towards the Gravitational Fields.

Retracing Steps

Retracing Steps is when our hands or fingers retrace ground they have just covered because something holds our attention and pulls us back. Once there, we usually need to vary between Stillness and Movement, going over and returning again a number of times until the area is at peace. As we Retrace Steps and hone in to a specific point, we are often naturally drawn to the Melting Pot technique.

Swirling the Mind

It is important to fluidly incorporate different directions in our work so the mind relaxes its hold and allows for a more three-dimensional sense of the body. Because the mind tends to follow the motion of the hands, Sacred Bodywork specifically encourages the use of techniques beyond straight lines up and down the body. Examples of this is the circular technique of Infinity, many of the techniques listed above and kneading. This swirling of motion is more difficult for the mind to follow and eventually it lets go.

Fine Tissue Work

Therapeutic Massage, Rehabilitative Massage, Injury Work and the Sacred Bodywork technique of Fine Tissue Work all work with aches, pains and injuries, and have similar objectives: primarily decreasing pain and/ or increasing range of motion.

However, these issues are not only physical issues, but disturbances in the energetic field in and around the problem area, as well as the patterns of disturbance they create within the mind. Therefore, we address the system as a whole rather than solely via the Physical Body.

Fine Tissue Work is the intricate muscle work applied to a small specific area that is in pain, discomfort or injured with the goal of diffusing and releasing its captured energy. When combined with other Sacred Bodywork techniques, this often produces a natural and gentle decrease in pain, discomfort and guarding, and an increase in flexibility and range of motion.

Areas of Tension

The professional must have a personal, rather than book-learned relationship, an actual rather than theoretical, understanding of tension. This relationship and understanding of tension (and the relief of tension) is achieved through self-awareness *and* the hands of another professional.

As we work with our clients, we honor each of them, are awake to each moment, to each touch and each person, working with and discovering where and how they hold, store, reflect and cope with stress.

In addition to the individuality of each person's tension dynamics, truth is also in the words of the client who states, "I don't need anything special, I just hold my tension in the same places everyone else does." The body *does* have common areas of tension and Sacred Bodywork integrates checking and working with these common areas of tension and dispersing the held energy.

Head

Most heads hold tension since they act as a storage and processing facility for thoughts, worries, plans, ideas, the past, present and the future. They can feel tight and even plastic wrapped or are so heavy laying in our hands that they do not move up and down or side to side.

Signs: Headaches and migraines. Areas of pain or discomfort to the touch. A lack of movement of the skin over the bones of the cranium. A sense that the cranium is not itself moving or breathing.

Often found in: Clients who have busy minds, those who are cerebral and overly use their minds to speculate, evaluate, study or plan, have Type A personalities, suffer from anxiety and worry or who have trouble letting go and going with the flow.

Temples and Forehead

Temples and forehead are often involved in frontal headaches from overused muscles associated with worry, anxiety, and a tendency towards over-thinking.

Ears

Ears tend to be tightly attached to the head due to fascial restriction, and with the temporalis muscle going all the way behind and in front of the ears, there can often be tightness and soreness. Unless the client has a headache, the restriction in this area goes unnoticed and the ears themselves disappear into the vastness of the body: a gentle ear massage can wake them up, fascia work with gentle ear pulling increases circulation and a sense of space and relaxation.

Bridge of Nose

Bridge of nose is a common area that people naturally rub, drawn there by the held tension. Simple long and circular strokes on the bridge of the nose can help with sinus problems as well as relieve tension in the face.

Eyes, Eyebrows and the Orbital Region

Just as the ears hear things they may not want to hear, the eyes see things they may not want to see. The muscles in this region are constantly at work as they change focus from near and far, working day and night as images and visions pass before them. Golden Butterfly Opens the Window, eye smoothing and cupping, fascial work, and using an eye pillow are all helpful.

Jaw, Chin and around the Mouth

Jaw, chin and around the mouth are all instruments of communication and emotional expression, and are affected both because we implement then so often and because we hold back what needs to be expressed. As we work these often-neglected areas, we make sure to work above and below the zygoma or cheek bones.

The Base of the Occiput

The base of the occiput often needs special attention and is often tight on those who have excess thoughts and difficulties stopping, relaxing and letting go. Melting can relieve tension and holding patterns, both physical and emotional.

Body

Neck

Signs: Stiffness, a reluctance or resistance for the neck to move with ease laterally or into flexion or extension, an uneven range of motion. This dynamic will be evident in the smallest of movements.

Often found in: Clients prone to headaches or migraines, those with whiplash history (even if it was many years ago) or arthritis of the neck. Also, in clients with surgically or arthritically fused vertebrae.

Approach: Melting each vertebrae and Melting the entire cervical strip in one hold are gentle and effective techniques. Working with the scalene and the sternomastoid muscles, although more intense, can be quite valuable. Intense work can be integrated into a session. Working the connecting area of neck up into the occiput and temporalis muscles can help to diffuse energy and tightness.

Warning: The neck always needs to be handled carefully and consciously. *Do not test for tension by turning the head to the side and pushing it into the table.* A client with a muscle strain, arthritis or trauma of the neck (including strangulation, blows to the neck and some cases of sexual assault or rape history) will stiffen up and guard even more. Professionals fearful about working with the neck can educate themselves by taking continuing education classes as well as by getting their own neck worked on.

Hands

Signs: Stiffness, fingers that are held straight and don't bend easily. Hands that are held in fists and don't open easily.

Often found in: Clients who get manicures, musicians, dentists and dental hygienists, surgeons, construction workers, plumbers.

Approach: Press down on the arms to stretch the muscles and ligaments and to bring circulation to the hands. Work on the entire hand including fingers. This work is usually fabulous for clients with circulation issues but may need to be applied gently and superficially with someone with arthritis in the hands or vein issues.

Arms and Shoulders

Signs: Arms that are held close to the body. Stiffness, particularly in the upper arm. Look for pain and sensitivity in the deltoids and biceps and ease of getting into the axilla, or area of the armpit.

Often found in: Tennis players, from repetitive impact and holding onto the racquet tightly. Sailors, from pulling on ropes. Musicians, from overuse of arms and hands. Dentists and dental hygienists, surgeons, from holding the same position for an extended period of time and from holding tools tightly. Construction workers and plumbers, from repetitive movements, impact (hammers and drills) and heavy lifting. Those who have had arm, shoulder or chest surgery often hold tension in their arms due to guarding. Those who were tickled as a child, even if it was veiled as fun—it creates a holding, guarding and tension response. Clients who have been physically restrained against their will. Women who are young mothers quickly develop a heightened awareness and are ready to spring into action, a dynamic that is expressed in the arms and shoulders (and reflected in a mind that has difficulty relaxing).

Approach: Press down on the arms to stretch the muscles and ligaments. Bring arms above head and work the shoulder girdle, axilla, deltoid, biceps, pecs major, infraspinatus, teres major, latissimus dorsi and serratus muscles. Sweep down past the hip for North/South work and/or into the ribs to affect the chest and diaphragm. Use Softening the Clay technique.

Pecs and Chest

Signs: No movement in the chest when client breaths deeply. Rounded back and/or shoulders pulled in. Collapsed or puffed out chest.

Often found in: Clients holding in emotion. Clients with asthma or lung problems, heart trouble, or those who have had chest, heart or breast surgery (including biopsy, lumpectomy, or mastectomy).

While both genders suffer from stress and heart problems, there has been no research that I know of linking physical chest tightness to heart issues, either as a precursor or a symptom. My guess is that research would find a chest that is hard, tight, restricted or lacks movement while breathing does nothing to promote a healthy heart.

Approach: Work on the pecs and sternum of both genders to loosen attachments. If you have both the client's permission and proper training, do a full chest/breast massage. Softening the Clay and East/West rocking at the ribs, shoulders and hips, and North/South rocking at the shoulders can gently help open the chest and rib area. The Under/Over technique at the chest or heart chakra is good for a client with sadness or an injured heart. Adding a gentle push up with the Under hand can increase breath to this area and an increased sense of openness. Spreading the arms out away from the body and off the table, supported by stools and pillows, can further open the chest and deepen breathing.

Stomach

Signs: Lack of movement with breath. Hardness that is not muscular. Pulled-in stomach. Sounds of digestion (which can stem from the system relaxing during the session, indicating it has been tense).

Often found in: Dancers, muscular people who have confused strong muscles with tight muscles and who cannot discern between the two. Those punched or hit in the stomach (boxers, martial artists, people in abusive relationships, those who were bullied as children).

Approach: Over/Under is a non-invasive approach. This can be coupled with Riding the Waves and Pushing against the Waves to increase relaxation of the stomach muscles. East/West effleurage and rocking, plus direct massage to the stomach. The stomach is an area that doesn't get enough touch in general. Our contact here must be confident and natural so we can give the client a more complete experience of their body and deal with the tensions that are held here.

Hips and Gluteals

Signs: Visible contraction and/or tactile hardening of the gluteal muscles on compression of the gluteal muscles. Imbalance in hip height.

Often found in: Skaters, dancers, yoga practitioners, pregnant women, golfers. Clients who drive for a living or who take a lot of flights. Clients who carry a wallet or keys in their back pockets. Clients who suffer from low back or sciatic pain.

Approach: East/West rocking at the hips, thighs, lower legs/calves and feet. This technique affects the hips in a gentle way and can be used to evaluate holding. Include direct work on the gluteal muscles, iliotibial band, piriformis, and hamstring attachments. Softening the Clay with the forearm can help them release.

Feet

Signs: Tension and stiffness in the feet. Feet that actively point (ballerina syndrome) even while at rest on the table. During foot circles look for feet that move stiffly or that resist movement.

Often found in: Dancers. Clients with arthritis or balance issues. Those who wear high heels. Restaurant waitstaff, nurses, retail workers, and others who stand a lot. Clients who have ticklish feet, those tickled as a child, those who say they don't like or want you to work on the feet.

Approach: Clients ask us to omit working on their feet for all sorts of reasons, including discomfort with the shape of their feet, dirty feet, foot or ankle pain, cuts, blisters, warts, ticklish feet, etc. Medical reasons are dealt with in a way that is appropriate to their condition. Clients should be encouraged to come to their sessions with clean feet and any open cuts and warts covered. Ultimately it is the professional's goal to 'normalize' the body by diffusing body image issues, and decreasing sensitivities.

Double-sided friction to the area of the ankle and foot directly or through the blanket, can casually loosen and increase movement. There are many foot massage techniques. Slow sweeping along each toe and in between the toes can give the client a more complete sense of the three dimensionality of their feet. Use Stillness, holding, compression and solid contact to minimize any sensations of tickling.

Legs

Signs: Taughtness in the tissue; no give. Hardness of the muscle unrelated to its strength. Inflexibility in the hips. Evaluate with East/West rocking at knee, hip and feet.

Often found in: Runners and speed walkers, postal workers, dancers, tennis players, skiers, airline personnel, dentists (technicians and hygienists),

Approach: North/South and East/West rocking and effleurage into hips and back. Softening the Clay and Fine Tissue Work.

The Use of Breath

Breath is an important vehicle of release of disruptions in the energetic matrix. For this reason, Sacred Bodyworkers monitor the breath for information while guiding it to be fully present in all parts of the body.

The breath is, conveniently, *always* present. Too often, it goes unnoticed and its potential to provide a sense of openness and release, unused. With gentle observation, it gives us a host of information, and with gentle guidance becomes an agent of change.

Professionals who become aware of breath also over time come to notice its connection to emotions, stress, pain, holding, and letting go. Once we have witnessed this connection, there is often a natural inclination to work with it.

If you watch a baby breathe, its whole body moves as its lungs fill with air. This is not something that should change just because we age. Life experiences can cause disruptions in the energetics of our system and change our breathing patterns and, in turn, affect our lung capacity. We may also be taught to breathe in a specific way (dancers and yoga practitioners in particular) and if we apply the teaching 24-hours a day, it often causes a disruption in our Physical and Energy Body.

Most disruptions in our breath are caused by emotional, physical or psychological trauma. We think of traumas as huge events but it's often those that have gone unacknowledged and therefore unattended that have a huge impact on our systems. What we work with as Sacred Bodyworkers, are these patterns of disruption, first noticing them and then encouraging them to shift into an unblocked, full, original and true nature of expression.

In response to any given incident that is traumatic to our system (a bad relationship, a difficult work environment, being yelled at, an injury, an operation, a scare), our brain reacts by protecting us, putting into motion a number of chemical changes (such as pumping adrenaline into our system) and physical changes such as increasing heart and breathing rates, blood flow, raising the chest and diaphragm which in turn restricts our breath, lungs and our hearts. In a prolonged state of stress, these changes can create a new set point so we are no longer functioning at our optimal levels, experience increased fatigue, irritation and altered behavioral and mood patterns so that any difficulty that comes along completely throws us off balance.

The Breath of Life abides in stillness and breathes a living fire that fashions creation. Nature's living breath weaves a trembling matrix that connects all living organisms to the free-flowing motion of good health. Breath is the mother and stillness the father, and together they create a polar process that organizes the wholeness of life. In this matrix, every subtle change in one part effects and modifies all other parts. The interconnecting fibers emerge out of a dynamic tension of opposites between unmanifest stillness and expressed form.

Life's web intimately resonates with your heart field; therefore, you cannot exist without affecting everything, and, at the same time, being affected by everything. Who you are, and what you think, feel, say, and do, creates tremors that modulate the tension in life's sublime threads. One tremor sets up another one that creates yet more motion, all of which constantly changes the tonal nuances in this intricate universal matrix, which in turn constantly evolves a new order out of ever-shifting chaos.

The eternal dance, in which chaos dissolves into stillness to express renewed order, *is* life. The Breath of Life unites us all—she contains us and she is in us, like a fish in the ocean—and life without her is preposterous.

Objects, situations, and living beings are not separate; the notion contradicts itself. Coherence means you resonate as a singularity *and* you are an integral part of the whole. Because your heart is coherent with all that is, when you let your life flow freely through you it is health. When you control life's

ebb and flow you not only stifle your heart, but, as Dr. Mae-Wan Ho, author of *Rainbow and the Worm* indicates, when life's "flow is interrupted, disintegration sets in, and death begins." Making choices that insulate you from uncomfortable experiences often causes you to collide painfully with reality.

CHARLES RIDLEY,
FROM *STILLNESS: BIODYNAMIC CRANIAL PRACTICE AND THE EVOLUTION OF CONSCIOUSNESS*

Rather than being at the mercy of our own biology and mind, during the quiet of a session we (both the client and the professional) can learn to use our breath as an agent towards physical, emotion and psychological health.

Notice any 'splits' in the body—if one side opens or moves easier with the breath than the other, or if there's a North/South split, which most often happens at the low back/sacrum, the solar plexus and the throat. A split is an energetic and/or emotional obstruction that separates, or *splits*, one part of the body off from another. If the split is at the low back, no breath will be felt there. It's more difficult to see the breath in the legs, but by no means impossible, a split may be accompanied by a heaviness of the legs. A split at the solar plexus will result in either belly or chest breathing, and a split at the throat will cause the breath to go into the chest but no higher, and the client's body may feel stiff and unmoving. This client may suffer from headaches and "spacey-ness" and the professional may observe that the head is heavier than they would have anticipated.

If emotional or physical discomfort or pain is present or triggered, how does the breath change? Does it deepen, quicken, constrict? Is there a sense of alarm? Do parts of the body tense? Watch for increased muscular constriction in the low back, the shoulders, and the buttocks.

Breath and Internal States

There are differing qualities of breath that reflect an array of internal states of mind, body or emotion: pain, sadness, grief, relief, a letting go, anxiety, held emotion, an openness... By observing breath in our clients and correlating it with the state they are in, we can learn to decipher its code.

Emotional states can be supported or calmed by our hands and presence. Under/Over can be grounding, nurturing and calming, and may also serve to facilitate release, as can using our own breath and/or guiding the client to use theirs.

Professionals at the beginning of their careers or with no tangential experience may be uncomfortable with emotional states. As a baseline, we need to be aware of any deepening of emotional states and, without shutting the client down, ground and calm them, honoring and respecting their process.

Your exhalation is a pressure release valve that allows stress, holding, tightness, thoughts, plans, and worry to accompany your exhale in its departure.

Breath can be a formidable stablilizer, keeping us fixed in a certain position or place forever.

It can also be a great force of change.

Breath and Release

Breath often acts as a pressure-release valve, accompanying an observable and palpable release, letting go and a deepening, as if held stresses have found their way out of the body and psyche. Muscles that were held and contracted let go and soften to the touch and parts of the body, or the body as a whole, visibly sink into the table. These releases are expressions of the dissipation of disruptions in the energetic matrix.

Visual Assessment

Visually observe where the breath goes, which parts of the body move with the breath, and which parts are rigid. Areas to pay particular attention to are the chest, stomach, low back, ribs and shoulders. Notice if they move as isolated parts or with the whole body. It can be more challenging to get a read on this while the client is sitting and talking to you, but it will give you a snapshot version of how their breath expresses itself and lives in their body. Keep in mind there is no diagnosis to be made, just a general impression, such as "holds stomach tightly, no breath going in there," "breathes into chest, but it's not going up into shoulders or past the ribs." Continue visual assessment when the client gets on the table and throughout the session. The body speaks, so what are their first breaths on the table saying and what do they say once you make contact with them?

Hands-On Assessment

When your hands are on the body, it should be possible to feel the breath at any and every location. Rather the hands being in a *doing* mode, they must be in a listening and feeling mode, relaxed, loose and at the same time, connected. The value of non-doing, of simply listening with the hands, is not only in the information we get, but also in the way it inherently leads the client to a more profound level of relaxation and deepening, as well as an energetic connection within the client and between the client and therapist.

What your hands and senses are looking or listening for is a full or subtle movement of lateral expansion and contraction and longitudinal elongation and shortening: expansion into the stomach and chest, a lengthening in the legs, a filling up in the shoulders.

Most often, the simple act of listening is enough to create a change in the client's breathing dynamics, and results in the breath moving into the very place your hands are doing the listening (similar to a baby in utero moving to the warm, safe, comfortable hands that are placed on the belly).

Guided Breath

There are clients who walk through our doors thinking about the traffic, parking, dropping their children off at school, if it's going to snow of rain, or the challenges of taking care of someone dear to them: the energetics of their lives are actively moving around their system. This is true for every client to one degree or another so beginning the session by reminding or coaching them to take deep breaths can help them settle in. It also gives you the opportunity to observe the amount and quality of their breath. As you guide them to breathe deeply, notice their response. What is a deep breath for this person? Where does it go and where are the constrictions, places where it gets stuck or splits?

Using Your Voice to Guide

To be a guide you need to have a goal and a destination. If you just say the words they will sound empty. There needs to be context. Watch the client's body and respond to what you see, guiding them to where they need to go to. Your voice will set a tone and rhythm that leads your client to a deepening state of relaxation, letting go and inward movement. Practice without the client being present if you need to so that you sound calm, grounded, confident and comfortable with what you are saying.

After you guide, observe. For example, you might say, *"Take some long and deep breaths, for now breathing both in and out of your mouth."* Now observe what happens. Notice how naturally the body expands or how difficult this is for them. Some clients will be uncomfortable opening their mouths to breath or may not realize that's what they need to do. Difficulty is an indication that further guidance may be called for: *"As you inhale, bring your breath into your lower back, expand it into your ribs (the front, the sides and the back), and all the way up into your shoulders."* The image of a balloon can be helpful; as it expands it fills up in every possible direction.

Observe again. What you are looking for is a slow expansion of the body with the inhale, and the easiest places to notice this is at the chest, ribs, stomach and the low back. You are also looking for the slow, deep release on the exhale. If you are touching them as you do this, you there will be a noticeable expansion and then a softening of the tissue with the exhale, an overall sense of them letting go, their body sinking deeper into the table with each exhale.

Each step of guided breathing can be the last as you move on to something different or it can serve as information for the next step. For example, next steps may be:

- direct the client to push their breath against the restriction they have become accustomed to in their body: *"When you feel you have breathed in completely, inhale more. Push your breath into your ribs and up into your shoulders. Now, slowly and deeply exhale. When you feel you have exhaled completely, blow the air out and completely empty your lungs."*

- *"You're lying down on this warm table, so gently remind your body that it doesn't need to do any work, your muscles and bones can completely let go. Each time you exhale, allow your body to get heavier on the table so that you let the table fully support your body."*

- *"As you exhale, start to allow your muscles to soften, to let go, and even allow your mind to begin to wander. You don't need to help, predict or problem solve. You can let go completely. If you start to drift off, allow yourself to do that."*

- *"Use your breath to open the places that feel closed, to soften the places that feel hard, to let go where there is holding."*

You can guide them to bring the breath into the areas it's not accessing or moving into deeply enough, or to places it needs to go to, such as a painful low back or tight shoulders:

- *"Breath is like a massage from the inside; it increases circulation and helps our bodies relax, so take a few deep breaths right into your lower back where you've been feeling that pain."*

This explanation is particularly good for those who think breath work is 'new-agey', and has no value and who are waiting for you to "get to the *real* work."

Using Our Own Breath

As professionals, we want to work with minimal physical stress on our own systems, and taking a deep breath, focusing on softening and letting go, can help us do that. Otherwise, we can be so deep in the session that an increase in our level of physical tension can go unnoticed.

When the therapist takes a deep breath, in many cases an automatic mirroring system kicks in and the client also takes a deep breath, so taking an audible deep breath acts as a reminder to the client to breathe deeply. This can be done at strategic moments, such as when working with pain, when you notice an increase in tension in the client, as a starter to the session or as intuition dictates.

This simple action fulfills the Dual Path by taking care of ourselves with the release of our own tension, while at the same time, gently and wordlessly guiding our client. Wordless guiding does not engage the client's brain; I find the client tends to try more when we verbally coach them to breathe than when they naturally and wordlessly follow our lead.

By using and becoming attuned to our own breath, we get to know the challenges our clients face; where restrictions can lie; how emotions, stress and pain can affect our own breathing abilities and patterns. On the Dual Path, it becomes about us, rather than about *them*.

Sound and Vibration

In my first few years of doing massage, I played the same CD in every single session. I theorized that doing this would condition my clients to go into a state of relaxation as soon as the music began, and for 98% of my clients, this is exactly what happened. I learned from doing this that repetition doesn't necessarily equate to  boredom, that it can create a sense of comfort and safety and can be a form of ritual, inducting clients into an easy deep state of relaxation. Since then, I have explored these themes of creating a sense of comfort, safety, induction and ritual, much of it through the senses: smells, touch and sound.

Music that Engages the Mind

If music engages the mind, it keeps the client present and their mind active, which is not the goal of Sacred Bodywork. Music should be an enhancement to the session, having a soothing and meditative effect for both the client *and* the professional.

- Classical Music: Although some clients may enjoy hearing their favorite piece of classical music while reading or relaxing at home, during a massage classical music tends to keep the mind engaged.
- Music that is 'catchy'. You don't want the client to be humming along on the table.
- Music with words in our own language can easily engage the mind.
- Sounds of the ocean, forest or jungle need to be excellently produced otherwise they tend to sound fake or repetitive, bringing attention to itself.

Music as Silence

It can be useful to think of your sessions as silent, using sound and music only to complement the silence.

Clients who are musicians can be particularly sensitive to this issue and often ask for silence over music.

Sound affects both the client and the professional, clearing the mind, setting the tempo for the body's system, and having a powerful transportive and induction effect. It is an integral part of the session.

Sound and vibration act like magic conveyor belts, ferrying away thoughts, worries, concerns, physical and energetic blockages and holding patterns. Himalayan Singing Bowls are ideal conveyors, and can be placed under, near or on the table as well as on the body itself to create powerful effects.

At our center, Hand in Hand, we keep a collection of sound and vibrational instruments, and will often use Himalayan Singing Bowls to begin a session, encouraging the mind to start its journey towards relaxation as it follows the sound. Whether near the body or placed on the body, the sound and vibration from these bowls can shorten the path from Earth to Heaven.

Do not use any sound or vibrational instrument in a session without first exploring its potential: I have heard tingsha bells struck in the most unpleasant way by those who either did not pay attention or who did not know their potential.

Do not buy sound/vibrational isntruments online; when you play or strike your instrument there is an interaction between it and the space it is in, between it and your body. It is advisable to spend some time in the store you are purchasing from, playing it, listening to it and getting information about it. We have been known to spend whole afternoons lying on the floors of our favorite stores, switching out one bowl after another, feeling which chakra center is resonating, listening for how it affects the body, mind and energetic matrix.

> Besides the natural charm that music has, it has a magical power, a power that can be experienced even now.
>
> It seems that the human race has lost a great deal of the ancient science of magic, but if there remains any magic it is music.

HAZRAT INAYAT KHAN,
THE MYSTICISM OF SOUND AND MUSIC

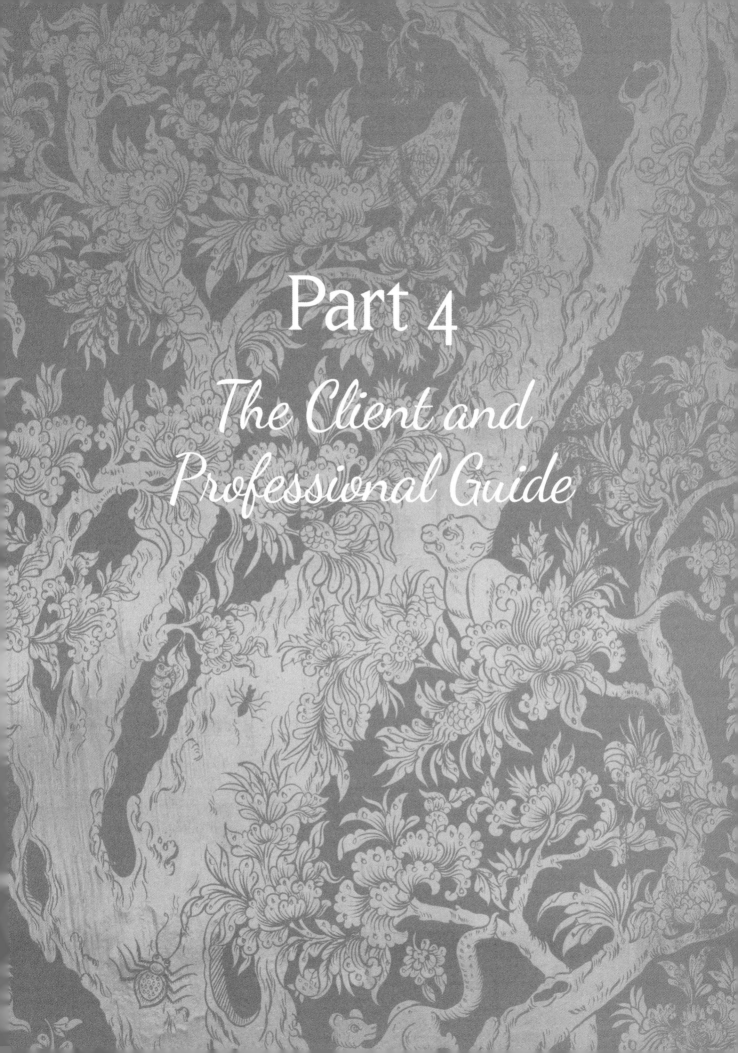

Part 4
The Client and Professional Guide

Opening the Door to Our Soul

This guide comprises information and tips for clients and professionals, and in total creates a guidebook that facilitates the journey from Earth to Heaven.

Some segments of this guide are geared specifically for the client or the professional. However, since the path of client and professional is a Dual Path, and all parts contribute and are intimately connected to the whole, I suggest you read all sections. For this reason, I have specifically not grouped them into their own sections.

Note: Some segments are not specific to receiving or giving Sacred Bodywork alone, but are beneficial for *any* bodywork client and professional.

Finding a Sacred Bodyworker

The term *Sacred Bodyworker* describes a way of working, but the terminology itself is new. Most bodyworkers work with the physical body or the spirit or energetic body, while Sacred Bodywork bridges the divide and *works with both at the same time* ferrying the client from one state of consciousness to another.

The goal of Sacred Bodywork is very specific, so you will need to be specific in your search. No two professionals are the same, so you may need to do some legwork, be precise with your line of questioning and even be willing to travel.

The professional you are looking for is a massage therapist, already working with and connecting to the physical body, who *combines* this approach with working with the energetic matrix, either having trained in polarity, reiki or craniosacral. They may also be proficient in Sacred Bodywork techniques, having mentored and/or learned them by video instruction or by taking classes at the Dual Path Institute.

When Looking for a Sacred Bodyworker, Find Out:

- What modalities they have training in. You are looking for someone with training at both ends of the bodywork spectrum.
- How much training they have and how long have they been working with these modalities.
- If they integrate these modalities. Many professionals may do reiki and massage but may do them *separately*. You are looking for someone who *combines* them.

- If they can help you *journey* or *travel* in your session. These are loose terms not taught in the typical massage program and most likely, only someone experienced in this facet of bodywork will grasp your meaning.
- If you are working with someone you already like, you may try introducing them to this book and ask them if they would be willing to add these concepts and techniques to their repertoire.

Other Search Tools

There is no one right way to find the right bodyworker. Every client responds in a different way and has different needs when it comes to bodywork—what is good for one may not be your idea of good. Even if someone describes their session, it doesn't necessarily mean that is how the therapist works with everyone, so although it is helpful to ask friends for referrals you will not know for sure that the match is a good one until you have experienced their work.

Organizations

Some massage professionals belong to organizations and can be located on the organization websites, such as:

- ABMP: Association of Bodywork and Massage Professionals—www.abmp.com
- AMTA: American Massage Therapy Association—www.amtamassage.org

These listings let you know who is in your area and which modalities they are trained in. It is the bare bones of who the professional is and how they work. If they have their own website, usually there will be a link to it.

Credentials

- LMT: Licensed Massage Therapist—licensed by the State
- CMT: Certified Massage Therapist—a graduate of a Massage Program
- LCMT: Licensed and Certified Massage Therapist
- NCMBT: Nationally Certified Massage and Bodywork Therapist. These credentials require the professional to get additional continuing education.
- BCMBT: Board Certified Massage and Bodywork Therapist. This level of credentialing is above and beyond National Certification.

It is important to note that none of the above are required by every state. In addition, credentials, an advertisement in the phone book or asking a friend for a referral is no guarantee of a good or even an ethical Professional. So, the following pages offer some guidance on how to proceed.

Your comfort level and instincts will help guide your decision. At the same time, your therapist should be:

- honest and respectful
- clear in their intention
- knowledgeable in their field
- working in a comfortable, clean, professional environment
- clear in explaining, setting and holding their boundaries

Good places to ask for a referral are often from those working in related fields: yoga studios, health food stores, acupuncturists, etc, where bodywork aficionados can often be found. Ask for a *personal* referral, a referral to a professional they themselves have been to. When you get a name and phone number, call them. Do not be surprised if you have to leave a message; many good bodyworkers are one-person operations and cannot answer the phone if they are in a session. They should, however, be responsive to your call, returning it, if they do not answer immediately, the same day or within 24 hours. If this does not happen, it may be a sign that they do not respond to situations in a professional manner, and that bodywork is more of a hobby than a profession.

Let them know why you are calling and ask them to describe their work. If they are stumbling over their response it may mean they are new in the field and haven't had to answer that question often enough. You should get a sense of confidence without any promises of possible outcomes (such as, "Sure, I can cure you of those headaches.")

Phone Questions

There are no specifically 'right' or 'wrong' answers. The idea is to get a sense of who you are talking to, what their level of professionalism is, what to expect if you decide to schedule an appointment, and see if it feels right for you. Here's some possible ground to cover:

How long have you been in this profession?

Proficiency in working with the energetic body takes time and it also takes a while once someone has graduated from a massage program to get away from following a routine and develop his or her sense of touch and intuition. Be aware that professionals who don't have a lot of experience may include their time in school in their response.

The benefit of experienced hands means that in addition to the massage feeling good, they will also be able to actually *feel* tightness and knots in your muscle, as well as know how deeply or lightly to apply pressure. They will have a larger toolbox and will be able to select from it as they discover what is effective and what is not. These are the skills that feel magical to the client, but in fact are just a matter of experience and tuning in.

As a rough guideline, under five years of experience most likely means they haven't had their hands on enough people. If the practitioner tells you they were in a related profession, find out what it was. Being a nurse, a doctor, a physical or occupational therapist may sound related to the layperson, but these professions do not advance their hand or Sacred Bodywork skills.

On the other hand, *there are* those rare individuals who have the natural ability to do this work from the get-go.

Do you have a full or part-time practice?

There are many reasons people have part-time bodywork practices. Here are a few I've encountered:

- They are aging or have been a bodyworker for a number of years and it came time to cut down on the number of hours they work.
- They teach bodywork or do something else that is related.
- They do other unrelated work, because they like variety in their life.
- Their interests vary and they don't want to, or cannot choose one to focus on.
- Their spouse is in the army and it's a profession they can travel easily with.
- They have children or elderly parents they need to care for.
- They use bodywork to supplement their income, rather than it being the profession of their choice.
- They are not good enough to build their business.
- They are hoping to quit their 'real job' but don't have enough massage business.
- They are afraid to depend on this work as their sole source of income.
- They have recently graduated from a massage program and are testing the waters, or haven't decided what their next steps are.

Just because a bodyworker is part-time doesn't mean they are not good or dedicated. On the other hand, it may mean exactly that. What a part-time practitioner means for *you* is that it is information to be taken into consideration as you gain a more complete impression through further interaction.

Do you work out of your home, an office, a spa, massage franchise, or health club?

The chances of finding a Sacred Bodywork Professional at a spa, massage franchise or health club is very small indeed. Those who work at massage franchises are most likely recent graduates of a massage program who would lack the necessary experience, while those at spa's and on cruise lines often integrate spa treatments and are encouraged to sell products. Health club massage professionals are likely to be focused on the physical aspects of the body rather than the spiritual. In general, those who work at these places often do so because they are in the early stages of their profession.

In addition, health clubs, spas, nail or hair salons often have odor and noise issues. Your practitioner will most likely be an employee and will not be setting their own schedule. Consequently they may be rushed, working with a schedule imposed on them.

If s/he is working out of their home, ask if they have a dedicated office. I have found homes to be a more likely venue to hear phones and doorbells ringing in the background, people leaving messages on answering machines and family members, guests and pets wandering into the room.

For some, these issues may be enough to look elsewhere; for others, it's just a consideration to put in the mix.

Other Questions You May Want to Ask

- Will there be paperwork to do?
- Do you take extra time for the first session?
- Is the check-in time included in the time of the session?
- Do you book your sessions back-to-back?
- What's your cancellation or late policy?

If you have a cold, illness, infection, allergy, etc. check in with them about your circumstances.

When You Meet

Are you greeted in a friendly, respectful and professional manner? Does the professional have good eye contact, hand shake and communication skills? Do they make you feel safe, comfortable and at ease? Use your intuition and common sense. Look for a clean room dedicated to massage and ready for your session. Notice if it feels clinical, messy, unprepared or cold.

Make sure you get a sense that this is a person you could both trust and respect. You may end up sharing personal information with this person and/or needing advice, ideas or referrals.

What to Look Out For

- Unreturned phone calls.
- Unprofessional boundaries in speech or body language. There should be a sense of care, compassion, even bonding, but no flirtatiousness.

- Someone who 'creeps you out' or who you don't feel safe with.

- Unprofessional draping techniques. Your private areas should be covered at all times, unless of course you have asked for and consented to a specialized form of work such as breast massage or you are in Hawaii on the beach or in some other setting wherein you choose to be naked. However, under these circumstances too, you should be treated professionally at all times.

- Communication that is one-sided.

- Someone hedging their explanations or using jargon you don't understand. If this happens, ask for clarification.

- Someone who won't spend the time to talk with you, or someone who talks endlessly.

Opening the Door to Our Soul

There are
many roads that
lead us to being a 'client'
—a gift, spare time, curiosity, stress,
illness, the need to relax, a doctor, a friend…
but most often it is our own physical discomfort.
Often we don't know we need and are
even looking for something deeper
but suddenly a map is drawn and the
landscape of our own body lays before us
finally, for us to see clearly, for all to see.
We look at it, sometimes with the vulnerability
of one who has never in fact been truly seen by
another.
We look at this new landscape like a blind person,
running our fingers over
not just the outer edges, but the inner contours,
the light and shadow within
discovering places of clearness and murkiness,
of heaviness and lightness.
Sometimes we raise our heads with tears,
sometimes with the shame of our own judgments.
As we progress, we learn that by being seen,
we are being honored;
that by seeing ourselves, we can become wise,
and that by quieting our own voices of judgment,
we can find peace.

In an effort to heal, we throw caution to the wind,
dig into our own pockets
often unwittingly opening the doorway
into our soul.

Getting the Most Out of Your Session: The Fundamentals

Give Yourself Enough Time

Make an event of it, giving yourself a lot of time and space. You don't want to feel or be rushed. Make sure you've dedicated enough time to find your way there, park, go to the bathroom, check in, take some time for yourself before the session to settle and connect to yourself, the session itself, check-out and most importantly, time to absorb your experience once the session is over.

Get Comfortable

Spend some moments before the session begins getting comfortable on the table. Make sure the temperature, head rest position, etc, is good for you. If you need assistance with any of this, ask as soon as your bodyworker re-enters the room.

Give Up Any Expectations

Don't expect a full-body session, or a particular outcome. You are probably looking forward to your session, and may be expectant of what might happen. Notice this and let it go if you can, using Finding Neutral, Returning to Neutral or your meditation practice if needed.

Don't Try

Your role is to relax and let go. That's all. That's not easy for everyone. Notice if it's not easy for you. Notice if you are anticipating what will happen next, or if you are trying to help. Your muscles and your mind should not be active. If you anticipate or find yourself having difficulty with this, let your professional know and if you find yourself not being able to relax in the session, let her/him know.

Don't Try and Be Present and Awake

This *trying* is towards a particular goal: trying to stay awake and present. Clients who do this usually do it for one of two reasons: they either don't want to miss anything or they feel they will not get the full benefit of the session if they were to fall asleep. Consequently they spend the session being alert and aware, and miss the point of Sacred Bodywork. Allow yourself to wander or be guided to a dream-like state. If you fall into sleep, allow yourself to go there. Not only will you still get the benefits of the session, but you will only get the benefits of the session if you stop *trying*. Don't *try* and fall asleep, don't *try* and stay awake.

Don't Chat

Having a meditative session and finding yourself journeying from Earth to Heaven simply cannot happen if you chat in your session. Don't hesitate to communicate whatever is important but allow yourself to deeply relax, to go deep. Even those who know themselves as *talkers* or who identify themselves as uncomfortable with being quiet can have a different experience. If this describes you, then this is your work; EFT can be helpful with this issue.

Don't Ask for Deep Work

Asking for deep work interferes with the intention of the session. The professional will use their judgment to ascertain the correct depth for your body and their goals. If, however, they use too much pressure, let them know.

Go Deep

Explore how deeply you can relax, open, soften and let go. Feel free to use your breath or to meditate during the session, but don't work hard at it.

After the Session: Absorbing the Sacred

This period of time is of the essence in Sacred Bodywork, equally important as the session itself as it allows your system to absorb the shifts in your energetic matrix.

Remain on the table once the therapist has left the room, returning to awareness slowly and gently. Get up when you feel ready, taking it slow, and then just as slowly, get dressed. You have been in another realm; do not jump from it into your life again as this abrupt shift can be startling and even traumatizing to your system. Your experience is in your hands to be nurtured. Plan this time ahead, knowing where you will go to honor the sacredness of your experience: a quiet and calm environment where you will not be interrupted. Begin by spending some of this time lying down, sitting or slowly walking with no particular agenda and when you are ready, meditate, contemplate or journal.

This is your job, to allow the formless to marinate, to saturate your very bones. Rather than coming back to who you knew yourself to be before getting on the table, move *forward* with this expanded and formless version of yourself. Don't allow it to slip away and become less and less real as your 'real' life solidifies you back into its previous shape. As your life enfolds around you again, you will need to look at the memory of your experience often. Treat it like the miracle it is, and reflect on its sacred nature. Spend the rest of the day practicing slowness, with not too much stimulation, social or otherwise.

Notice how you feel: Lighter? Heavier? Dreamlike? Spacey? Open? Honor these wonders and appreciate them for the miracles they are so they will visit you more often and more easily. Your meditation practices and your bodywork sessions will begin to work hand in hand, the cumulative effect taking you to the sacred cauldron of transformation.

Beyond the Fundamentals

Before You Arrive

When you book your session make sure the professional you are seeing knows that you want Sacred Bodywork, otherwise they may proceed with another modality.

Showering makes for a much appreciated contribution to your session; make sure to clean your feet from any sand or dirt so it doesn't get all over your body.

Turn your phone off completely *before* **you arrive for your session or leave it in the car or at home.** Think of your session as beginning the moment you walk through the door, if not before. You will want to be looking at your therapist when you meet or are talking to him or her, not at your cell phone, so turn it off before you walk in the door. You also want to avoid the struggle of bringing your attention from whatever is going on in your phone communication back to the present moment, or feeling that connecting to the person in front of you is a disturbance, an intrusion to your phone activity.

If your phone is with you, make sure it is completely turned off. When we are deep in silence, a dream state, or anywhere else in Heaven, our energetic matrix is in a state of fluidity, and while in this condition, rings, buzzing or beeps can be hugely disturbing, abruptly shocking, and cause a negative rather than positive shift in our energetic matrix.

Once You Have Arrived

Arriving twenty minutes to a half hour early allows you time to sit and get still, to be with yourself, to breathe and perhaps to contemplate or meditate. If a waiting room is not available, a car works just as well.

Check in with yourself and your bodywork professional. If you arrive for your session preoccupied by what you have just been doing, or by what's going on in your life, notice this and let your bodyworker know. Take some time to connect with yourself and what you need. It is often helpful to take a breath, close your eyes and evaluate your internal landscape, describing your state of being to your therapist.

If you feel you're not really in touch with yourself, it could be a sign of disconnection, that you are overwhelmed or that a deep river is running through you. To connect with what is riding on and under the water, close your eyes and like a meditation, notice what comes to you. If you are nervous, afraid, blank or exasperated by the idea of doing this, don't feel obligated to do it. Let it go.

Where you are and what you need may be as simple as wanting to relax or feel rejuvenated. Perhaps something has been draining or stressing you. Are you dealing with a time of change? Do you have aches, pains or injuries that hound you? How have you been sleeping and dreaming?

Even though you may be in tune with your needs, remember to let go of any expectation of what will happen, how deep the work will or will not be or what areas of the body will be worked on. Communicate to your practitioner what you are aware of, and leave the details of the session up to them.

On the Table

The less you do, the better. If you don't know how to do that, don't worry; it is just a matter of relearning something your system has forgotten. Know that you are in the perfect place to do just that.

Experiencing the spirit, the formless, cannot be achieved unless there is full and complete relaxation of both body and mind. This level of relaxation is not like spending time with a favorite book, participating in a creative endeavor, listening to your favorite piece of music, going fishing or spending a day or week at the beach with a drink in hand. Although it is true that there is a degree of relaxation in these situations, we are aiming deeper. We are aiming to experience any number of the Heavenly states that connect us to spirit. It is here we are reminded that we *are* spirit, that we *are more vast* than the form that reflects itself back to us in the mirror, that our spirit has nothing whatsoever to do with our weight, hair style, blemishes, the character we have come to know with its concerns, anxieties, thoughts, emotions and behavior.

Any workings of the mind or body during the session are an impediment to this level of letting go, and for many of us, this path means retraining ourselves to get out of the way.

Notice if:

- Your mind feels busy
- You feel very aware of what is happening
- You feel anxious
- Your body feels like it is *holding*, arms held close to the body, fingers *held* straight, etc.
- You are anticipating what the massage professional will do next
- You helpfully adjust your arm or leg to where you anticipate the therapist wants it to be
- You are holding your breath

These are signs of a mind that is too active and/or there is fear of completely letting go. As you notice these dynamics, treat the realization like a dragon visiting you in meditation, gently acknowledging their presence and letting them know that at this time, they are not needed. Remind yourself to relax, take some deep breaths, focus on softening the places that are holding and encourage your body to sink into and be held by the table. If this continues to be your challenge, let the massage professional know *and* address it in your EFT sessions.

You Are Not Deeply Relaxed When You...

- feel very awake
- talk or your mind is active, thinking, worrying or planning
- are physically uncomfortable
- are uneasy closing your eyes
- are jumpy, fidgety or keep adjusting your position
- adjust your arms to get them out of the way or put them in the position you believe the therapist wants them in
- are nervous, anxious, worried or concerned
- want to do it right or make a good impression
- feel tense or stiff
- feel your body resisting as the massage therapist moves your limbs, head or any other part of your body
- need to know where the massage therapist is
- get off the table quickly
- check the time or your phone as soon as the session has ended
- start thinking about your responsibilities as soon as you get off the table

Why Is This List Important?

Many people do not recognize the signs of tension and have become habituated to them, ignoring them for so long that they become part of their identity. Most of us were not taught how to relax, or that it's something we need to learn and practice, and we're certainly not taught that relaxation should be a priority. Some people are tense, even during a massage and when they find themselves more relaxed at the end of a session than they were at the beginning, they are content and believe this is as relaxed as they are able to be. Many of us have systems that simply do not know or have forgotten how to get to a *deep* state of relaxation, and what this state feels like. A deep state of relaxation is not only possible and available to any one, but both necessary and advantageous to health.

What Can the Client Do to Achieve a More Relaxed State?

- Give yourself permission to completely let go, to be taken care of and nurtured. Use every opportunity to explore how deeply you can relax and let go.
- Accept that trying to help your practitioner in any way will keep you from your goal of deep and systemic relaxation.
- Get completely comfortable on the table before the session begins.
- As you lay down on the table, breathe deeply through the mouth, as if you are sighing and use the exhale like a pressure-release valve. With each exhale allow your body to get heavier on the table as your muscles and bones start to realize they don't need to do any work. Rather than being like raw spaghetti, you want your body to be limp, like cooked spaghetti.
- Allow your thoughts to settle, like mud at the bottom of a lake, as the comforting sensation of hands contact your skin. Drift into the flow of their movement over your body.
- Follow a dream state if it comes to you. Don't stop yourself from falling into sleep.
- Let your practitioner know this is your goal
- Meditate

Despite all this guidance, don't work hard!

Giving the Best Session: The Fundamentals

These fundamentals are applicable to Sacred Bodywork and almost any kind of bodywork. The unfortunate reality is that I am not alone in having received many sessions where the fundamentals were lacking.

Before Your Work Day Begins

- Showering and using some form of deodorant before your workday is an absolute necessity. We work in very close proximity to our clients...
- If you have a qigong, yoga or meditation practice you should have already done your practice before work so you will be focused, calm and grounded.
- Arrive early so you are ready. Make sure your workspace is clean, organized and smells good. Check your music, room and table temperature and make yourself tea or pour yourself some water so you can stay hydrated.

The Workers of Magic

We are the
workers of
magic,

a gentle hand
supporting the journey
forward and inward

allowing for transformation
of thought,

body

and life itself.

We are the people who touch.

We touch the skin,

the wounds,

the energetic field,

we touch the invisible

and we touch the lives of those around us.

We are a creature who

within ourselves

have opened the door to other realms,

the realms of the ancient

and the realms of the scientifically miscomprehended.

We wander, invisible,

having been touched ourselves by the Sacred,

having been ever so subtly, and ever
so profoundly, transformed.

This is our profession,

to dip our toe,

even slightly,

in the world of the shaman,

to be the current that propels

those we touch

on their Sacred journey.

Client Arrival

- When your client arrives, greet them warmly and make them feel welcome. Have them complete any paperwork and if you can, spend some time in informal conversation.
  - If they are early, show them where to wait; offer them water or tea and show them where the bathroom is.
- Once it is time for the session, you should not be harried, looking for this or that, doing one *last thing*. Everything should be ready, and your time is theirs.
  - Chat privately in the session room before they get on the table, your eyes and ears tuned in to where they are within themselves and what they need.
    - Give them relevant information, including how you will end the session and what they should do afterwards.

Table Work

- Re-enter the client room focused and present.
- Your first contact is intentional.
- Stay relaxed in your mind and body.
- Sight can override our other faculties. Periodically close your eyes to drop in deep and awaken and absorb through your other senses.
- If you notice tension in your body, breathe and invite yourself to open, soften and let go.
- If you find your mind is busy, use the Sacred Practices that are applicable and helpful, such as Returning to Neutral and Meditation.

- Be present in your touch. Using touch as your Return greatly enhances presence. Return to the sensation of your hands on their skin, to what you feel beneath the outer layer, and/or what you see by acutely focusing your vision where you are working.

- Take deep audible breaths at suitable times to remind the client to breathe, or to facilitate the client's process of opening and letting go.

- Use good body mechanics so you stay grounded and connected so that you don't put strain on your own body.

- For Sacred Bodywork, begin the session with sound and vibration by using a Himalayan Singing Bowl on or around the client's body to lead their mind on its journey. End the session the same way, so as to bring the client gently back without using words, which in contrast will bring them back too fast, pulling the mind into the present to pay attention.

- After the session, spend whatever amount of time is appropriate with the client. Do not expect or encourage them to describe their experience to you. In fact, doing so may disrupt their state.

- Remind the client to spend at least an hour alone, absorbing their experience.

- Rather than immediately starting another session, take some time for yourself in between sessions. Use this time to clear your energetic field: sage the room, meditate, journal, make some tea, lie down…

How Long a Session?

Due to the meditative nature and goals of Sacred Bodywork, sessions are ninety minutes or longer.

Chair Massage to Hone our Skills

Chair Massage is said to have been invented in 1986. It is often taught as a routine. It is also promoted as a marketing tool, the main points being that the professional can get exposure to a lot of people in a relatively short amount of time, there is no need for oil, customers don't have to take their clothes off or commit a lot of time, and often it's free. It has a lot of selling points. In addition, Chair Massage allows the professional to be an educational resource for the community where people can ask questions about bodywork, your business, and what they are experiencing and needing.

In Sacred Bodywork, Chair Massage is a challenge, and challenges help us grow. It's a venue we can use to explore particular techniques such as Melting, and how to quickly lead the client to a deep state of relaxation. These short sessions can also serve to improve and test our intuition, and hone our sense of presence and connection.

Once children learn that their parents get bodywork, they often become curious and want to share and understand their parents' experience. A shared experience such as this can create a common language and expand the child's resources.

Half-hour sessions may be perfect for children. Sacred Bodywork is particularly effective with children who have suffered a loss, a trauma, are hyperactive, or who have been diagnosed with Attention Deficit Disorder.

The use of sound and vibration, such as Himalayan Singing Bowls, is often a source of intrigue and has a powerful effect on children's sensitive systems. It is not unusual for a child to start out as squirmy or stiff on the table even if it is their choice to be there. They will achieve a deeper sense of comfort and state of relaxation with each session. Sessions with children can be done fully or partially clothed and with the parent seated in the room. These choices would depend on the age and state of the child along with the wishes of the parent. We've also had the occasion to do these sessions with the parent holding the hand of their child on the table and other times where both parent and child are each on their own table in the same room.

Children may also be brought in for their own health concerns:
- A 12-year-old with two concussions, bad knees and a bad shoulder.
- An 8-year-old whose father had died of cancer.
- A young girl with a bad back facing being dangled above the stage as Peter Pan.
- A young boy with lower back issues after being tackled while playing Lacrosse.
- A young girl suffering from headaches every day. Her mother said all her daughters' friends complained of daily headaches too. One massage and she was headache-free for weeks while her friends were not.
- Kids of all ages with bad backs and shoulders from carrying enormously heavy backpacks.

Having been in this profession since 1991, we've witnessed that children who get massage tend to grow into adults who feel they have a larger toolbox with more choices.

Hour-long Massage, a Popular Choice

An hour is the average and most popular amount of time for most clients. Those who know how much better a longer session is often book an hour so they can assess the professional, returning for a longer session if the experience was good.

In Sacred Bodywork, an hour risks dramatically compromising the essence of the session. An hour can be successful if the needs of the physical body are not extensive, but In essence it is still a compromised session.

Fifty-minute sessions are increasingly the choice of a spa or franchise because it allows them to start their sessions on the hour, without wasting a lot of billable time in between. Since this pace doesn't promote professional longevity, it is not usually the choice professionals would make for themselves.

90-Minutes or Longer

This length of time has a powerful advantageous affect on the tempo of the session, creating a deeper state of relaxation that maintains itself for a longer period of time. It's that simple. It's that profound.

Some people ask their friends, "How can you lay there for 90-minutes?" Our clients ask, "Why would you want to get up after an hour?"

Create a Comfort Zone

The comfort zone is a behavioral state within which a person operates in an anxiety-neutral condition, using a limited set of behaviors to deliver a steady level of performance, usually without a sense of risk (White 2009). — Wikipedia

You want your client to find themselves in their comfort zone the moment they step through the door. However, it is not enough to *want* the client to feel at ease and be comfortable; we must take an active role in creating a Comfort Zone.

Noticing and learning from our own experiences of comfort and discomfort, being attuned to what might cause discomfort, the ability to read its signs, to be relaxed and natural as professionals, all contribute to creating a Comfort Zone. Without *comfort,* the client may find it difficult to feel safe, to let go, and *be* comfortable.

In creating a Comfort Zone we must consider the:

- Welcome
- Level of organization, familiarity with the process and focus of the professional
- Conversation
- Temperature
- Physical comfort on the table
- Privacy and confidentiality

The Welcome

Clients and non-clients alike have told us they make a point to walk past our business, look in the windows, and soak in its calming effect. Those who walk into Hand in Hand say they feel relaxed the moment they step through the door. So when does the session begin?

The welcome includes everything that greets your client: scent, sound and sights and will be their first step into a world they will be glad to continue to visit. This world should be calm, confident and beautiful, with a splash of mystery hinting at the journey to come.

In life, we are bombarded with sights, sounds, and smells, so a subtle, calm, and relaxed environment is better than overt when it comes to the senses. While being subtle, they are still powerful, invisible forces that actively and warmly welcome them each and every time.

The scent should be warm, subtle and good rather than a reminder of a hospital, laundry room or a candle store. The sound should be some light background music and a warm, welcoming voice rather than a ticking clock or a voice full of anxiety because they are late. The sights should be thoughtful and meaningful; the client should not see clutter, dirty linens or professionals dressed in scrubs. What they see should allude to the journey they will be going on.

Our place of work is often multifunctional. We not only see clients, we also do paperwork, have lunch and hold meetings. It is easy to become accustomed to a slow build-up of papers and clutter. Make sure to look around, periodically assessing through all of your senses and re-beautifying your environment.

Professionals are taught to be professional, rather than personal, and that may translate as cold and distant. Being professional does not erase our humanness, nor should it. If the connection is warm, real and sincere, *you*, not even your work, will be a good association and memory. If more than one person walks through your door, be thoughtful around gender-bias. Some professionals still hone in on the female as if she is your only potential client.

Saying, "May I help you?" can make people feel like they have walked into a department store. In a department store this question makes sense because the shopper may need to be directed to a department, but in a massage business, there is a short list of what they are interested in or curious about: you, your services and your rooms.

Some years back, I painted toilet seats that I displayed and sold in art shows and fairs. I called my business *Monique's Uniques*. I quickly learned my medium encouraged conversation that I had no interest in: bathrooms, bathroom decor and bathroom habits! You need to have a true interest in all aspects of your profession because it is from this that your curiosity and ability to connect stems.

The year President George W. Bush was up for re-election in 2004, was a time when there was a great deal of hostility towards Americans and Blane and I were on vacation in France. We walked in to an art gallery and when the owners realized we were American they warmly welcomed us, invited us to sit down, talk and drink tea with them. We stayed a good long while, chatting about the election, Americana and our travels. We still remember that connection and kindness all these years later. That's what you want to do with whoever walks through your door: be human, warm, natural and welcoming.

Dealing with Stress, Anxiety and Difficult Situations

Any number of situations may be a source of stress, frustration, irritation or anxiety for either the client or the therapist. For example, if the client is late they may feel disappointed, irritated or upset at the prospect of not getting a full session or stressed from whatever caused them to be late. Meanwhile, the therapist may feel pressed for time, anxious that they cannot give the session they had hoped in the shortened timeframe, and torn as to whether to end the session on time or go over time. This stress can be inadvertently expressed in our voice and body language, causing a client to become even more stressed and even feel unwelcome.

Clients who are short with us, impatient, irritated or even rude present a special challenge.

A person in this state may illicit negative feelings at their place of work or in other areas of their life, but in Sacred Bodywork, these difficult states simply identify the grain of sand stuck inside the watch, the disturbance in the systems functioning. These states show us the client's particular energetic imbalance—not to judge, like or dislike, but to illuminate the demons that call to us to help them slip silently into a heavenly state of calm.

A client who *constantly* presents as grouchy, rude or mean indicates blocked and stagnant Earth energy. This energy may clear and diffuse to a certain extent within the session but their life is set up to reset the pattern. However, this client is prone to return, enjoying and needing temporary relief. These clients often feel that change is impossible and are overwhelmed with the prospect of working with Sacred Practices. Unfortunately, if they are not on the Dual Path working with Sacred Practices, the pattern will most likely continue for the rest of their life.

The therapist must be particularly clear when working with these clients so as not to get pulled into or mirror the client's state, voice or behavior. If the therapist feels unable to cope or remain clear, feels mistreated, abused, traumatized, scared or treated cruelly it indicates the need for one or a combination of the following: supervision, setting boundaries, ending a session, terminating with the client altogether, asking a client to leave or referring the client elsewhere.

Organization and Focus

Once your client arrives and it is time for their session, your focus should be with them. If you are fumbling around trying to figure out how to take payment, how to check them in, where the paperwork is and how to fill it out, the process becomes the focus.

When working in a new environment, familiarize yourself with how the headrest and music works, where supplies are kept, what paperwork the client needs to do, the ins and outs of the room you are working in. That means arriving early, figuring things out and/or asking questions and taking yourself through the steps of what you need to know. It is not professional to fumble through, figuring these things out with the client: you will come across as distracted and unfocused and rather than going into gear as soon as the client enters, you may find nothing going particularly smoothly as one gear grinds against the other.

Conversation

When I first began doing bodywork, it was not for the conversation, it was for the lack of it. I was drawn to bodywork because it bypassed conversation altogether, instead going straight to, what I intuitively felt even back then, a deeper and more authentic connection and truth. However, time brought with it conversational ease, and a discovery that these face-to-face moments permits each to see the other's earthly presence, integrity and intention, allowing our connection, and therefore my contacts, to begin earlier and go deeper.

Although conversation fulfills a number of necessary functions for both the client and the therapist, it also has the potential to feel invasive or time consuming. Throughout your verbal interchanges, be sensitive to the client's tone of voice and level of engagement. Be ready to facilitate going inside, straight to the core, through bodywork.

Tone of voice is an indicator of the state of mind, your own and your client's. For the professional, it is not enough to have a neutral or positive tone of voice if inside we are unsettled, irritated, exasperated, demanding or judgmental. File your reaction away for later exploration. EFT can be particularly helpful with this.

Topics of conversation are like a suitcase being unpacked, each item contributing to the whole of the picture of what the client carries within them. If the therapist is doing all the talking, is it the client's suitcase we are unpacking? On the other hand, we do not have the same boundaries as psychotherapists, whose general ethic is to never talk about themselves. Conversation should be natural and balanced.

The Dual Path honors the parallel paths of massage therapist and client, understanding it is only the details of the scenery that make the journeys different. The Dual Path knows that we are kin, not different creatures, and that by *sharing* the struggles and difficulties that have crossed our path, the ensuing empty compartments of our luggage serves as a reminder of the natural order of things—that we each face obstacles and challenges, that each person wields their own sword and slays the dragon that bars their way. Nevertheless, here we stand, on the path together.

Temperature

I often remind the client that it's *their* session, not mine nor that of the client prior to them: a room or table that is too cold for one may be too warm for another. A full day of clients will probably find you adjusting the temperature to suit each one while you adjust to their needs with layers of clothing you can put on or remove. You will come to know those who have hot flashes, those who need the extra blanket, the heat on the table *and* in the room, and the ones who run so hot they never need a blanket and even want the sheet folded down, uncovering their back, and up to uncover their feet.

Prepare the room temperature before the client arrives. In general, the room should be cool in the summers and warm and cozy in the winter. Air conditioning, table warmers, extra heaters and blankets are all basic tools of the trade. A bottle of warm or hot drinking water or a cup of tea can double as your hand warmer, and heated oils can feel fabulous on the client's skin while adding warmth to your hands.

The bottom line with temperature is to make sure you ask; make sure they know the temperature is set for *their* comfort, not yours; and that you have what you need to respond to their needs while also accommodating your own comfort level.

Physical Comfort on the Table

With a new client, begin by giving a little information on the workings of the headrest, informing them that you will help make adjustments so they are comfortable once they are on the table. When you return, smooth any ruffled sheets, adjust the bolster and headrest, and actively support and encourage the client into more comfortable positioning. As the session progresses, pressure and techniques may cause a change in the client's comfort level with the headrest. Fidgeting and repositioning may be indications that adjustments need to be made, that your set up is not comfortable, or that the client needs to turn over.

Client Comfort on the Massage Table

As professionals, we have very few tools and necessities; oils or lotion, sheets, headrest covers, hand sanitizer, that's about it. Even music is not a *necessity*. The massage table is different: each and every client lies on our table each and every time they have a session. It is our most important and valuable tool, and yet I have used headrests that forced my head and neck into the single available position, giving me neck pain and headaches. I have been on tables so hard they actually caused pain to my sacrum and breasts. Even if the therapist's work is amazing, I would not consider putting myself in such physical discomfort a second time.

How comfortable can you make their time on your table? What is the most comfortable table on the market? As you get massages yourself, assess the comfort level of the table and headrest and then peek underneath to find out what make and model they are.

Professional Comfort with the Massage Table

Your table is not only the primary source of physical support and comfort for your client, but a major contributor to a short career or professional longevity. In school, we're told to adjust the table for each client, but most of us know that doesn't make any sense. If you've never met the client, how do you know what height to adjust it to? To adjust it once they are in the room is time-consuming and looks unprofessional. Even if we know the client and can predict that we'll need to adjust the height of the table, most of us don't take the time to do so.

This premise addresses only one facet of this issue. The other is that the table height has equally to do with *us* as it does the client. The height of the table also relates to the part of our body we are using to apply our technique, hands, elbows or forearms, so that we optimize leverage and decrease strain. If we decide to sit or stand, again the height of the table needs to change. Being able to adjust the table to the optimum height for specific techniques (such as placing a knee on the table near the clients head to drape their arm over), or to use as a support for a hand or a knee, or to lower it if we want to get up onto the table itself, is extremely valuable.

With a hydraulic or electric table, the table height can be changed at any time with no disruption to the flow of the session. There are a number of these tables on the market, so make sure you get a good sturdy one, not necessarily the most affordable. Try it out—there's at least one on the market that tips when you sit on the end. This piece of equipment stands out as the most important tool you'll ever buy for yourself; with the touch of a foot pedal it lowers the table to help a pregnant woman or a client with a back injury more easily get on and off the table, while saving your body years of accumulated unnecessary discomfort.

Along with the table comes the head rest, or face cradle. There are now numerous headrests available with three possible adjustments: height, angle and pad, and still there are professionals who use headrests that are completely un-adjustable. If you've ever tried on a piece of clothing labeled as "one size fits all" you know what I'm getting at. You don't want clients dreading being face down, getting jaw and head compression or headaches due to the pressure. Even with these completely adjustable headrests I haven't found one that is the perfect choice for every client, so we have several brands on hand. If the client just can't get comfortable, we can switch them out.

Privacy and Confidentiality

Knowing what they tell you will be private and confidential will help the client relax and feel more comfortable even if they don't share any personal information. Work towards creating a reputation for yourself as someone who honors this code of conduct, even stating it when needed, such as when you are seeing members of the same family or both parties in a relationship.

Massage and bodywork therapists often have a professional code of ethics laid out by the licensing state, an organization they belong to or a certifying body. This code of ethics usually contains requirements about confidentiality. It's a good idea to post it as a declaration to your clients. Privacy and confidentiality is no small thing:

"My worst experience was when I was going to someone who I thought was professional and would hold my personal opinions confidential as I was on their table. I said something in confidence to that person and less than 24 hours later it came back to me. Not only did it come back to me, they took it out of context and put their own spin on it. Needless to say I never went back to that professional again." — Patricia

The Importance of a Sickness Disclosure

The Sickness Disclosure pertains to honorable standards that contribute to neither the client nor the professional feeling worse by the end of the session.

We all know enough about spreading sickness that we should do what we can to prevent our clients leaving sicker than when they walked in, which is what I've seen happen when professionals with colds, flu and bronchitis work rather than taking time off. It's not particularly pleasant to have any professional, be it a dentist, optician, chiropractor, massage professional or anyone else, sniveling, sneezing and coughing all over us. For many, if we are not working we are not earning, which is why colds and flu spreads so rapidly in office environments.

Many Massage and Bodywork professionals work with clients struggling with immune deficiencies or treatments that suppress their immune systems (such as cancer treatments). If we work with a client with a contagious illness, they may spread their germs to us, and we may inadvertently spread them to those who may not be able to cope.

Some clients may not realize that have glassy eyes or a stuffy nose or that these are indications of a cold while some may believe that their cold is negligible but over the years, many clients with nothing more than a slight sore throat have gone on to a full blown flu that they and their whole family have come down with.

Establish a Two-way Disclosure Policy

Offer your clients the option to reschedule when you are sick. If you are under the weather but not sick enough to take the day off, disclose your situation and give your clients the option to go ahead with their session or not. Nurses and teachers of small children, and others who spend a lot of time around sickness may have strong immune systems and never get sick themselves.

Ask your clients to assess their health 24 hours in advance, to coincide with a 24-hour cancellation policy. Suggest they have a back-up person to send in their place in the event they find they are sick and don't have time to honor your cancellation policy.

Be clear with your clients about what you consider to be 'sick,' since people measure this in such different ways. We have had clients call to cancel because they have a head-ache or their back hurts—perfect reasons for actually coming in for a session.

For us, *sick* is any symptom at all of cold or flu and most cases where clients are on antibiotics. If a client is dealing with cancer, depending on where they are in their treat-ment and recovery, they may need a letter from their oncologist to let us know if there are any contraindications.

A client taking antibiotics is fighting an infection. Whether massage can spread infection has been an ongoing topic of conversation in the massage world. Be aware that any infection or possible infection near the head, such as in or around the eyes, strep throat or pre or post-root canal surgery can travel to the brain in no time. The topic of antibiotics suppressing the immune system is a less discussed topic but can be explored in the resources listed below.

Although not enough research is available, it is always best to be safe rather than sorry. It is helpful to be able to offer the client an alternative under these conditions, such as a Craniosacral session, Sound and Vibration sessions or EFT.

Read *Beyond Antibiotics* by Keith Sehner, MD and Lendon Smith, MD. and articles listed in the Internet Resources section.

First I felt the therapist's
breath on my face.

It was light at first

and then slowly,
it came heavier and heavier.

I was about to tell her
it was unpleasant

when her head
dropped onto mine.

For a moment,
she had fallen asleep.

Don't Breathe On Your Client's Face, and Other Advice

Falling asleep on a client is rare, but less rare is the therapist's breath on their client's face and this alone can be uncomfortable and disruptive to the client's experi-ence. Fortunately, there is only one position where this is an issue—seated at the head of the table when the client is supine.

Some therapists cope with this by turning their head to the side while they are working but over the long term this can result in neck problems similar to those clients who cradle phones between their neck and shoulder.

The other option is to breathe through the mouth instead of the nose. Just take a moment and put your hand in front of your mouth and nose. Take a couple of breaths and you'll find that if you breathe through your nose the breath comes out like a laser beam and is much more focused on wherever your head is pointing, while breathing through the mouth diffuses the air.

Anatomy books say there are four pairs (eight total) of muscles for mastication (chewing) while Visionary Craniosacral therapist, Hugh Milne, discusses the sixteen muscle groups attached to the mandible, and 136 muscles employed in chewing, swallowing, making expressions and kissing. To keep the mouth closed, there's an awful lot of constant muscle contraction.

Neither the lips nor the teeth should be touching. If either the top and bottom lips or the top and bottom teeth are touching each other, muscles are in contraction. You don't need or want to hold your mouth wide open. Just relax your jaw and lips a little so there's a small, almost imperceptible gap.

Like all habits that need to change, it just takes practice to form new, healthier ones. Just keep bringing your mind back to your breath, like a meditation, relaxing your jaw and slightly parting your lips.

Hair Up or Down?

The head is the gateway to thought, worry, tension, anxiety, problem solving and patterns of holding. However, when we focus our work in this area with Fine Tissue Work, Systemic Relaxation, Craniosacral and energy-oriented work, the head becomes the gateway to transcending those states. To facilitate this work, hair should be free-flowing and free from any restrictions, including pins, hair barrettes or bands. Outside of a session, these types of restrictions of the hair and scalp should also be minimized since they can contribute to a host of problems, such as increased tension and headaches, as will overly tight glasses and hats.

Massage Oil vs. Lotion

Many of us have become diligent with the oils we put *into* our bodies, choosing from a variety of available oils for cooking or salads.

When it comes to putting oil on the body, we must be just as diligent. The oil most commonly used by massage therapists is Sweet Almond oil, which has a tendency towards thickening and stickiness, and is a powerful allergen. Allergic reactions range from itching and rash to more severe and even life-threatening reactions.

Switching to a lotion has its own set of problems: they can absorb the smell of the plastic they are usually bottled in, and are often heavily laden with additives, preservatives and fragrances, causing a similar allergic reaction.

Many professionals still use whatever they used in school. It is important to be educated about any toxins we may be massaging into our clients skin and into our own. A high quality oil is not only a good medium, but is also nutritionally beneficial to the skin and hair.

My recommendation is organic unscented jojoba oil (pronounced ho-ho-ba) or organic coconut oil. Both have a long shelf life, are highly nutritious for the skin and hair, absorb well and are pleasant smelling. However, we have found jojoba to be less available and more expensive.

Taking Off One's Clothes

For a Sacred Bodywork session, all clothing should be taken off, including underwear.

So much of what we wear fits at or around our waist, physically and energetically disconnecting our upper from our lower body. Removing everything allows the massage strokes to reconnect the upper and lower body (North and South poles) to create an integration and reintegration of the whole body. When we connect the two hemispheres, there is an increased sense of wholeness and relaxation.

There are a number of reasons clients may want to keep their underwear on:

- Some clients have never thought about it one way or another
- The client doesn't know what they should do or what the expectations are
  - They are uncomfortable with the idea of being naked
  - They are uncomfortable with their body or outright dislike their body
  - They only take their underwear off for sexual activity or to take a shower. Their relationship to taking their underwear off is so connected to their sexual life that they keep them on for a massage so they don't 'give the wrong impression,' or 'get excited'.
  - Women who are afraid of 'spotting' on the table
  - Male clients who want to discourage arousal
- Clients with abuse histories

Some of these clients just need to be informed what the goal of their sessions are, and what is to be gained by

Bring your strengths to your profession,

because clients are going to bring their vulnerabilities

changing their mindset and choosing a different path. For others, deep levels of relaxation need to be experienced or trust may need to be established before they can forgo their immediate discomfort so as to allow for long-term and systemic gain.

For Rape and Abuse Survivors

Those with a history of rape or sexual abuse may go through a period of being uncomfortable taking *any* clothes off, so to take off underwear would be a big step. This completely normal phase must be honored.

At the same time, it is important that the client know that this traumatic experience which may have caused a daily disruption in their relationships, body, lives, spirit and energetic matrix *can be cleared over time, given the right professional bodyworker.* In fact, many survivors come to bodywork with exactly this as their goal and intention.

Our history is not something that needs or is supposed to live within us in the same way forever—we are not fixed in stone. There is an invaluable payoff in working towards change in a way that is gentle, caring, supportive and un-traumatizing. Sacred Bodywork and EFT can be a powerful duo in these circumstances.

Touch.

It all comes down to touch.

The essence of this work is that we are replacing, hmmm, displacing

a negative experience of touch with a positive one.

Please remember this.

This is our foundation:

We replace negative touch with positive touch.

Don't lose sight of the simple commitment

to deliver touch with loving kindness.

REBECCA MAE BACON

HUGH MILNE, FROM A CD TITLED, *UNWINDING*

Professional Attitudes

In most western massage, and likewise in Sacred Bodywork, the professional never sees the client completely naked.

Wherever the session takes place, whether in a home, office or a hotel room, the setting, attitude and behavior is professional. An appointment is an unwritten contract that no sexual advances will be made by either party, no flirtation, no admiring looks or comments. That doesn't mean that the conversation and touch will be or should be cold or disconnected. In fact, this clear discernment by both parties allows the touch to be whatever is needed in the moment: warm, comforting, nurturing, and/or treatment oriented, without fear or anxiety and most importantly, without having a negative influence on the energetic matrix.

"I take them off, it just seems like the right thing to do. It's more comfortable and relaxing. Keeping my clothes on would just not make the massage feel right. Once I am under the sheet I go into a comfort zone that is hard to explain." — Robert

"Naked, please! I want the therapist to be able to touch skin wherever he/she thinks necessary to de-stress my body. I'm not thinking that I'm at a massage parlor (as synonymous with brothel) but rather in the hands of a trusted professional." — Kalo

"By taking off my underwear I feel freer to relax knowing the massage won't be interrupted by clothing." — Roberta

"I normally take my underwear off. Over the years, the joke has been that I would rip my clothes off to jump on the table for a good massage! I feel pretty comfortable with massage and the therapists I go to. There has been only one instance where I did not take my underwear off. It was an energetic thing—the therapist creeped me out." — Patricia

"Naked is the way to go. I do with either gender masseuse and have always done it." — Rob

"What is the point of wearing undergarments during a massage? To me, that would obviate and frustrate the purpose of the body work. If the masseuse can't reach certain parts of the body, then the treatment would not be fully effective. Further, wearing underwear would seem to be an American cultural more, smacking of the antithetical body image and body consciousness Americans hold. I've never understood why Americans have such an issue with nudity whereas other cultures simply accept it as a part of living and life itself. A good masseuse is trained in acceptable touching. The purpose of the massage is to treat the body, spirit and mind." — PJ

"I take my underwear off. Taking my underwear off makes it easier for the massage therapist to move their hands over my body." — MSR

"I always take my underwear off. It allows for more freedom. Over the years, I have had so many delicious massages: it gets easier and easier. If you have excellent practitioners of massage that you come to trust, eventually you walk to the session dressed in sweats with no jewelry and no underwear just so you can be less restricted and get on the table faster." — Liz

Comfort and Safety

Clients come to our doors in all states of need, in need of relaxation or with an injury, and with their own past or present stressors or traumas. Before we can help another, the therapists own need and history must be healed, or at least, put aside.

Although we take note of any reaction we have to a client, we put it aside to take note of something else: the response we get when we silently ask what their deepest need is.

Through the simple act of compassionate listening, caring and touch, and no more than that, a client enters the treatment room in one state of body, in one state of mind, and often leaves in another, transformed. This transformation, often a sense of grounding, of wholeness that circulates within their system, leaves with them. The more they experience this, the more familiar they become with these strengths, their strengths, the closer that day comes when they no longer need reminding.

What we offer is a sanctuary, a place where people can take off the outer layers of what they carry around with them, and be at peace, deeply letting go, or venturing into discovering themselves, opening doors that may never have been opened. The container for this cannot be contaminated.

Gender and Attraction Issues

This is one profession where people often explicitly state a gender bias, saying things and asking questions that wouldn't be acceptable in most other professions: *"Is Blane a man? I don't want a man!", "I'd like a girl." "How old is she?" "Is she pretty?"*

In a Sacred Bodywork session, as in any bodywork session, factors such as gender, age, attractiveness and sexual orientation should not play a role for either the client or the professional. The professional is chosen for their ability to be clear and present, for the quality of their touch and, in Sacred Bodywork, for their ability to transport the client. It falls squarely on the shoulders of the professional to be professional, to be the guide they have been hired to be, to stay connected to their core.

In Sacred Bodywork, these issues are addressed by using some of the Sacred Practices and are understood in the following ways:

Attraction disrupts energy and any disruption, whether it is stress, anger, attraction or anything else, is a sign for us to connect more deeply with our core, or to Return to Neutral. *Anything* that pulls us away from our core, or neutral, is not seen as important in itself. Our practice of Returning to Neutral is one of the most important practices of all. Speeding up this return to neutral, accompanied by the development of an increasingly speedy realization that we have migrated away, is one of our life's goals. In Sacred Bodywork, this allows the client not only to relax more deeply on the table, but to more easily step on to the conveyor belt to Heaven. For the therapist, Returning to Neutral allows our energy system to remain intact so we focus fully on our work.

These thoughts or feelings are visiting dragons. Notice they have come to visit and invite them to leave, watching as they fly off. This calls for a strong meditation practice.

For those who have been emotionally or physically hurt, or who have felt threatened or made to feel unsafe by a particular gender, creating safety is natural and healthy. In the context of bodywork this can drive someone to seek a professional of the opposite gender. However, what is a natural and healthy phase in our healing can easily become a lifetime of self-protection and guarding, clouding our lives with anger, resentment and a closed, protected heart.

Ultimately, we long for a sense of internal freedom and joy, which is the destination of the paths of Sacred Bodywork and Sacred Practices. This is where Practice Session #8, Finding Your Compelling Vision can guide you, by seeing where you are, the direction you are heading in and making a sharp turn when you can towards the best possible version of yourself.

Liking What You See

It is not an uncommon fantasy for clients to want to date their massage practitioner and despite it being in violation of massage professional ethics, it does happen. I have also come across massage practitioners who view their profession as an opportunity to meet a dating partner. I cannot say enough about the damage these behaviors and attitudes have on our profession and on the individuals involved.

Some say that it is only human nature to be attracted to certain people. As professionals, we must be aware of our own hearts and longings, and neither project them onto our clients nor feed into a dynamic that needs to be healed. We must realize it is up to us to be clear and to step into a place of gentle understanding that leads the client back to their core, to a place where they can heal any wounds they are operating from.

To be influenced by our own needs, desires, or a client's 'good looks' blinds us to the truth. Perhaps their looks are the bargaining chip with which they gain attention and love. We may neglect to see that their looks have led them to feel deeply unseen, or misunderstood or mistrusted. Perhaps they've felt they can't go anywhere without being looked at and judged, so they never feel quite safe or secure. It is our job to open the envelope and see beyond what is before us, to see what is present, not with our eyes but with our open hearts.

As a Sacred Bodyworker, there is no scenario where the client and the professional have anything but a professional relationship. What options are there for the professional or the client who feels attraction?

- It is not professional for the practitioner to share their feelings of attraction with the client. However, the client may discuss their feelings with the professional, knowing that an ethical professional will not respond to any advances but will consider this information to be part of what contributes to the clients energetic matrix.

- The client can consider switching to another professional so they can focus on what brought them to Sacred Bodywork. They may also consider staying and working to diffuse this disruption in their energetic matrix.

- If the professional cannot stay focused on the therapeutic relationship it indicates they must work to clear their own energetic matrix through the Sacred Practices, including using EFT with a professional. Rather than causing harm, they should terminate with the client.

The Ritual of Creating Comfort and Safety

The professional's hands, words and actions create a sense of safety and are an integral part of the journey of health and healing. It is the professional's job and oath to honor this role their client has bestowed on them. If you are in the wrong place within yourself—untrained, immature, needy, unprofessional, unprepared, inexperienced or all of the above, the client will sense this and not feel honored. If the client does not feel honored, no healing can take place, only a re-experiencing and re-enlivening of their embedded patterns and dynamics, including potential retraumatization.

The client and the professional are co-participators in this ritual, creating safety through a clear and yet unwritten contract:

- After the check-in, the therapist leaves the room.

- The client does not begin to unbutton, pull at or take their clothes off while the therapist is still in the room.

- The client undresses and gets on the table *under* the covers.

- The therapist knocks and returns to the room.

- The professional ritual includes naming the table a massage *table* and not a massage *bed*, again desexualizing the experience and bringing clarity to where you are and what will and will not happen.

Feeling Unsafe

Even if the session has already begun, both the client and the professional have the right to stop the session.

It is not a good idea to get a massage on a cruise, in a hotel, in your home or someone else's if you have never had a massage, don't listen to your intuition, don't feel safe or suffer from anxiety.

I had blocked my listening and visionary skills for so long.

Then it came to me.

My listening skills and visionary perception returned.

The healer becomes the observer watching the client who truly is the healer.

They both wake up,

from the place of no mind, heart centered spaciousness and love.

They move in and when it is time, they place their hands in contact with the other's body,

knowing they are not only touching the body.

The bones and muscles may begin to tell their story.

That which was locked up in the body can begin to breathe.

It doesn't need to stay in the back, the unconscious, it has a place now.

And when something is met, truly met,

it is almost as if it never existed at all.

COURTNEY DUKELOW
WWW.COURTNEYDUKELOW.COM

How do you know where the pain is? Is it magic?

It doesn't surprise people that a carpenter can see the problems in their house even though to them their house looks fine. But people have this idea that they live in their body, that they've had this body their entire life, so how can someone else know anything about their body that they don't know?

Because this dynamic is already set up in their psychology it sets up an idea that they're hidden, but they're only hidden to people who don't look, don't see, or who aren't trained to do both of those things. So, when they are shocked by the fact that we can see or feel something, or determine where the edge of their pain center is, or how much they can take, or what they find uncomfortable, what they find most uncomfortable is that they feel exposed. They feel like this should have been hidden, and it's not. And so it comes out like "How did you know?" And we know because it's what we do. It's our profession. If it's a hobby, you may not know. We've certainly seen a number of practitioners who aren't able to distinguish between scar tissue, a fatty cyst and a tight muscle tissue, they just don't know the difference, either because they're not really invested in their practice, or they don't have very good training or they're just not very perceptive. Those people are out there. And oddly enough, those people may not give a bad massage, but that does not make them, in my terms, a good Bodyworker, because they can't see below the level of the skin, they can't see within the body. And what makes a very good practitioner is someone who has developed a sort of x-ray eye, to see within at different levels, and to see how those different levels are interacting, rather than remaining blindly on the outside of the body and pushing over the skin.

In western society we have stripped out most of the activities that allow us to develop a deeper sense of communication. We do not often have long conversations. We have gone from a story-telling culture to to a book-reading culture, from a book-reading culture to a television watching culture, from a television watching culture to a computer culture, and from a computer culture to a phone culture. All this has done is stripped us at each stage of that contact which we need in order to have a smooth back and forth interaction.

People say there's more communication now between people who are texting. Okay, of a certain type, that is true. Is it better or more subtle communication?

No, it is not. Because our ability to learn, to communicate non-verbally is far more powerful, and far older, it's millions of years old, stretched across every species on the planet, except ours. And we have it just as much as they do—it's a birthright. But if you don't practice it, it's like a language you learn when you're young, but you never speak again so you lose it.

It's like we've taken our peripheral vision away and have left ourselves with tunnel vision. The tunnel vision might be sharp but it leaves out all the nuances of the grays and the patterns, which we are able to pick up but we have forgotten how. So the idea that someone else can look at you and see all these different things seems extreme.

It's only really a matter of how much we get out of our way, and how much of our ego and agenda we can put aside in order to hear what the body is actually saying to us. We need to take that moment of silence to hear. That's the purpose of meditation, that you become silent enough in yourself so that you can hear your own inner voice in its actuality, unfiltered, unrestrained by our own desires or needs.

Blane Allen in Mongolia, 2004.

How to Listen

Without honing this skill, the professional cannot achieve their primary purpose.

Slow your movements down, as if you are moving through mud. At times, stop all movement and just become an antenna, a radar detector, a receptor. Listen for what the body is trying to communicate to its owner, what it's trying to communicate to you.

On the surface you will notice the quality of the skin, any tautness, dehydration and systemic inflammation. Underlying that is the fascia, the muscle. Is there strain, contraction or activity, such as jumpiness? Allow yourself to ponder if their system has been neglected, overused, overworked, over pumped or over stressed.

Listen to the breath. Can you hear anything, feel anything? If not, is it because they're so deeply relaxed? Or are they holding their breath out of habit, because they are hyperaware or fearful? Is it fast or slow? Listen to the speed and quality. Are there sighs? Are these out of pleasure, boredom or letting go? Listen too with your heart, what does their breath say to you? What story does it tell? Use this information to connect, not to judge or react to, just to connect.

Watch and listen for the twitches or jumps under the skin, or perhaps in the fingers or an arm, or a hip and contemplate where the epicenter of this movement is, what was being held there and what is being released. Listen not only to the parts, but the whole. Listen not only with your parts, like your hands and fingers, but with your whole system. Listen by relaxing, by letting go of doing, by allowing yourself the opportunity to develop x-ray vision.

Challenge yourself to be ever more present. Be in your body, in your hands, in your fingertips. Are you thinking about dinner? Come back to the session. Are you distracted by a sound you heard? Come back.

Feel yourself make contact. Feel the contact between your hands and their body. Listen for the movement right there under and in your hands; the temperature, rhythms, content.

Can you be with this touch, and this one, again and again, over and over? Practice. Every session, every moment. The sessions, the moments will come again and again.

If in the last session your mind wandered, or was so busy you couldn't even track it, resolve to be present in the next session.

Every session, and every moment within a session is an opportunity, a meditation where you bring yourself back to the breath or to the mantra. Bring yourself back to the moment.

Feel and listen to the stillness within you and the sacredness of the moment.

Being present does not mean being hyper aware or alert. In fact, being deeply relaxed or even sleepy can intensify our sense of presence. Explore different states of mind as it relates to your sensing ability and how shifting your state of mind relates to that of your clients.

The Parts or the Whole

Around my fifth year in this profession, I had a new client who stated that most practitioners work on each body part separately, which leaves the body feeling like it's made up of separate parts. I felt pretty confident with five years under my belt, so I did my best to 'mix it up' but overall, neither one of us were very impressed. I scheduled a meeting with my then mentor and told him the story. He told me that the best massage he'd ever received was from a woman who rarely did long straight strokes: her foundation was not with straight lines, but circular motion.

After my own exploration, I found that each has its own value and effect. While circular techniques can affect the mind like an on/off switch, long full-body strokes help create a sense of wholeness and connection between areas of the body that are often not connected, such as the lower and upper halves of the body. These long strokes can have a meditative and contemplative effect, relaxing the body and the mind.

Working together, the two approaches help us work with the body as a whole rather than on the parts of the body. When we become aware that we have been working on the arms and now we are working on the legs, we must check in to see if we are stuck working on the parts rather than the whole.

We often look at each part of ourselves as an independent piece of the whole—is it smooth, wrinkled, blemished, dry, oily, aching, stiff, or flexible? It is sometimes necessary to work on the parts, but our role is to help the client connect with their wholeness.

Taking Our Cues from the Client

Most people come in and, to one degree or another, tell us what they need. "I just need to relax…" often means they don't really care which *parts* of their body are worked on, they just want to have a relaxing *experience*, which refers to the *whole* of them, mind and body. If the same person adds that they have a headache, or that they and their spouse just decided to get a divorce, or they've been working out a lot and are feeling tight all over, it would change the tenor of the session and where the time is spent. The person with the headache would most likely get more time on, or perhaps exclusively on, their upper body, and we may also choose to work at the feet to pull the energy down. The client going through a divorce may get more work around their heart chakra if there's a lot of grief; their head if there's a lot of anxiety; or their feet if the energy needs to be grounded. The person who worked out and is stiff all over would most likely get a full-body session, with more focus on areas of energetic stagnation. Whatever area or *parts* of the body is worked on, our focus in Sacred Bodywork is to have the client leave with a sense of their wholeness.

Some people have areas of the body they *love* to have us work on, commonly the feet, face and head. Areas that people know they *need* work are commonly shoulders, neck and low back. Areas that people need work on but don't know it include the face, head, glutes, chest and stomach. All these preferences and needs are to be taken into consideration.

Bodies, Not Burgers

Some people believe that a *real* massage is a full-body massage, but bodies are not burgers; no two bodies are the same, and no body is ever the same from one day to the next. It's a matter of tuning into the parts *and* the whole, being present to what's calling to us and what needs to shift—not a prescription or a pre-made plan.

A Sacred Bodywork session is fluid, the hands flowing to where they are needed and where they are called, staying as long as there is a gravitational pull, responding to the bodies' living tissue and the entire system of the energetic matrix.

May each and every session be true to your unique body.

Personal Revelations

Texture and sensation have always been a source of intrigue to me; the feel and the sound that travels through the air to my ears and through my body as my foot slowly and consciously crushes dried, crunchy leaves in the autumn; how flowers, leaves and grass on my fingertips give or hold their place under my gentle touch; the dips and curves, smoothness or roughness of hair, skin, walls and sculptures.

The act of touch itself seems to capture a moment in time and adds a vital dimensionality that is otherwise missing. Moments can pass all too quickly, and touch calls that moment to us and allows us to savor it like an amazing strawberry.

Sacred Space and Transformation

From the first moment of contact, I listen for the crunch of the leaves as my hands fall into place picking up the rise and fall of breath, texture, dips and curves, smoothness and roughness. In so doing, sacred space is invited in and the call for transformation goes out.

As we narrow our focus on this link between matter and energy, Earth and Heaven, the system of transportation between the two and the transformation it affords start to unfold.

As dreams, emotions, behavior, and thought patterns seep into our awareness, we discover this is not just about touch, but an opening of an energetic doorway.

As there is progress along a personal path, so too does our work progress, these paths becoming extensions of each other, like twins sharing observations, explorations, learning, deepening and growing in tandem.

Heaven Shakes the Foundations of Earth

Lying on the table is a breathing, feeling, heart and soul. I'm not referring to the *person*, the person is another matter in itself, but the *being*, with its eco-system of internal noises and movements, its vibrations and frequencies, its winds and waves of shifting energies and its occasional volcanic explosions and shifting of tectonic plates.

Our hands and fingers, rather than *doing*—holding, pressing, turning, grabbing, kneading, and tapping—*feel* and *listen*, becoming receptors, listening devices, alive and soulful.

As these listening skills deepen, we witness the disintegration of the thin veil of character, circumstances and experiences, revealing a far deeper and more dynamic potency: the rivers, lakes and oceans that express life force. First, there is a softening of the edges, as if something is going out of focus, and then a melting as they slip into an amorphous state of suspension with its own universe of flow, tides, ripples, waves and undulations. As we gently hew their internal landscape, slipping and sliding in like a perfect and natural fit, we discover that we in fact can coax and lead them into this sacred space.

All of us, to some degree or another, live a mundane life. We do whatever *needs* to be done: work, clean, cook, eat and take care of children and parents. In other words, we all walk this Earthly path. But each of us, according to our individual natures, searches for, seeks, yearns for the magic, the dream, the hope, the otherworldly: Heaven. In a quiet moment we willingly let go of the self we know, the solid ground we stand on every day, and slip and slide into a place where we fly high or soar deep within, or just catch a glimpse of a self that is self-less: One-Who-is-Spirit.

At this point, One-Who-Washes-Dishes-Cooks-and-Cleans has an awakening. Their awakening may be a small moment or a huge cavern, and it may hold their attention or go unnoticed. Even if it goes unnoticed, something has begun to shift, the ground has begun to move and rumble as Heaven shakes the very foundations of their Earth.

In a quiet moment,
they too,

willingly let go of the
self they know,

the solid ground they
stand on every day,

and slip and slide into
a place where they fly,

transforming
Washer-of Dishes into
One-Who-Is-Sprit.

Part 5

My Sacred Journey

Sacred Life

If we honored the sacredness of life we would not have 16,306 species of animals and plants threatened with extinction.

If we honored the sacredness of life we would not have a history of turning human against human, torturing and bombing each other, enslaving, raping and murdering, wiping out civilizations, polluting our air, water, land and even our own bodies.

But this is not the tale of our history; this is the reality of our current behaviors. We cannot concede these atrocities as being inflicted by foreign invaders, by aliens or by armies. These are the behaviors of individuals; people just like you and just like me.

As individuals, each one of us has the capacity and the potential to be the protector of the spirit of each and every life, not only by refusing to participate in outrageous atrocities, but by reshaping our roots so that we honor the sacredness of all that lives.

As a species, as individuals, it is up to you, to me, to each one of us to remember and to teach future generations that *life is sacred*.

ﻊ

I learned much from my parents and the world they lived with and how they suffered from their experiences long after the war had ended. Although I did not learn from them how to live a sacred life, I did come to my own realization that *life itself is sacred*.

A Buddhist nun once looked me in the eye, saying, "*Always* have compassion in your heart."
Always
is in every moment,
every
single
moment.

My parents met in romantic Paris after the Second World War. They never told me their love story but my sense is that the romance was subsumed by the immense stress of their experience. My mother, born in France, survived the war by being in hiding in Paris while my father, born in Czechoslovakia, was taken along with his family to Auschwitz, and emerged with his sister as the only survivors. Not being able to get a work permit in France, my parents applied for visas in other parts of the world. They were admitted to Australia where my two brothers were born, Australian citizens. Later, my parents immigrated to England, where in 1960, I became the final addition to the family.

Due to their childhood war experiences my parents lacked formal education. They worked hard—my father as a factory worker, my mother selling French perfume and cosmetics in department stores.

My parents survived with life-long cases of PTSD and as a child I was aware of my father's tormenting nightmares, feared his rages and was deeply saddened by my mothers bouts of despair. I myself had such vivid nightmares of Nazi's taking my parents away that during the day I hatched plans of escape. As a young girl I was riddled with grief and desperation and as a teenager the only mentorship I had was to study hard and be strong. I staggered into life, never having the opportunity to be taught the lessons my parents were themselves deprived of. I was my parents' daughter: as I recognized that I bore my father's pain and my mother's anguish, I understood that my emotional and psychological growth had been stunted.

My mother, Rosette Eisner, daughter of Szulim and Jeanette Hochberg, February 14, 1929 – June 10, 2013.

Even though they tried their best to shelter their children from what had happened to them, it was as if their life experiences were mine. I myself was lost, or had never truly existed to begin with.

My parents loved my siblings and me deeply, but their experience had left them in survival mode and they parented in the only way they knew how, shaming us and raging at us in an effort to control and shape us. They expected their children to be strong, to be fighters, and couldn't bear to see signs of fear or vulnerability. Any sign of tears, sadness, fear or vulnerability marked us as weak and sensitive—responses that did not have a place in the world they had grown up in. To ensure our survival, we became hardened, unable to breathe through the thick walls of our defenses. This pressure-cooker life became part of my very fabric, and although I left home when I was sixteen, I continued to prove that I was a fighter by applying this pressure to myself.

The dysfunction and sickness of humanity that had created the atrocities of the Holocaust had also created dysfunctions in my parents and in myself. Even though I understood, I was also horrified to witness my parents emergence from their experience with an unequivocal xenophobia for Germans and Arabs and any nation that stood by. Later in life, as a therapist and a self-defense instructor, I witnessed a similar cycle in my students and clients: fears, anger and other reactions were often universalized and passed from one generation to the next, held in the system of both perpetrator and victim, and completely disrupting the potential for growth.

I vowed to break the cycle, to clear myself of the legacy that had disrupted, distorted and completely overwhelmed my true nature. I was exposed to a world that stood by, that continues to stand by and I vowed not to. As a witness to each of the members of my family, coping and surviving in whatever way they could, I vowed to take a hand in shaping myself and discovered that with work and dedication I could move forward as if born anew. In the process of doing this work for myself, it became clear to me that with guidance anyone could achieve the same results. It also became clear that we as a species must be committed to doing the work, to the Dual Path, which is both personal and global growth.

The rare and treasured moments when my father had a special glint in his eye as he told us stories of his mischievous youth, my mother's laughter and the way she loved to dance, and their fierce love for their children revealed the potency of the spirit they would have had if their spirits had not been crushed so long ago.

It is this potency of spirit, the undying seed at the core of every one of us, which even after the most dire experiences shone for me like a beacon and has guided me to find my own sacred path and to the awakening of my own spirit.

A Spirit Awakened

I realize that most people don't have my story—each one of us, our lives and journeys, are unique. However, we do have these truths in common: we each struggle to connect with and honor our sacredness and in every moment of our lives we are faced with the life or death of our own spirit. Possibly this truth scares us more than the death of our physical body, because when the spirit has been battered, its damage is visible for all to see in a life un-lived, bitterness carried, a body withered, a soul tormented, a person lost, life wasted, eyes glazed or turned in, the heaviness of shame and guilt, the darkness of misery, the secrets that come alive at night or in moments alone, the sadness we bury, the anger that bursts free from its hiding place...

Like most people, I didn't recognize that my spirit was in jeopardy, I just knew I felt desperate and hopeless, lost and alone. It was from this place of desperation that I began the fight for my life and for a spirit that otherwise would have died, leaving me empty, lifeless, and soulless.

I both looked for and blundered into opportunities for insight and change, eventually finding the right ingredients that drew me into their vortex. On my path, I discovered that no amount of strength, focus or willpower can defeat the old stories, habits, beliefs and pains held in our body, psyche and spirit. I discovered that the actual truth of personal transformation comes about through purposefully working to awaken and set free our spirit.

The results of the transformation are that I, and my life, have changed so drastically that I find myself surrounded by people who believe I must have been blessed with my current disposition. They often believe that I am fundamentally different, stronger, calmer, and more focused than they. However, the power of my story, the truth of it, is that although the details of my personal story may be different, I am no different than most everyone else. I did not grow up in an enlightened family, learning compassion, yoga and meditation. On the contrary, for many years I was blinded by pain, bitterness and anger, the energetic matrix I inherited from my parents.

As we age, most of us measure life by what has been lost and this could easily have been my own measurement. With an awakening of the spirit, rather than a life marked by loss, it's path is one of presence, filled with renewed vitality. It's a beautiful thing to choose to blossom, to grow, to transmute from the difficulties and heaviness we carry with us into a lightness of being and a fullness of heart. This is the spirit awakened.

My life has led me to a spirit awakened, a journey that lays the foundation for this book. Your life has led you to the convergence of our paths and to your own personal vortex to awaken and liberate *your* spirit.

May you honor the forces within and around you.

May you live with meaning and joy.

May you be true to the sacred within.

Wake-Up Calls

We all have wake-up calls. As you'll read further down, the channel we went to see says, *"If you look deeply into what's been moving you, [the wake-up call] is an internal feeling of, "Is this all there is?"* I would say if you are reading this book, you have heard the call. For some, the call is the little voice in the head asking, *"Is this all there is?"*, for others it is a baseball bat on the head, a divorce, an illness, a tragedy. Some of us need to hear it many times or need the forces of the universe to come to our aid, helping us find our path and throwing our lives into a new trajectory.

Anyone directly or tangentially involved in a war, any one who sees their life flashing in front of them, anyone who is a survivor has felt the pressure to wake-up, to do something meaningful if they survived.

Fortunately for those who are looking to heed the call, there are increasing resources pointing the way to awaken our spirit, save ourselves and save the world—including this book, written with those very goals in mind.

اللّٰه

My life has been a series of wake-up calls. The first was being born to Holocaust survivors. The others ranged from the persistent voice in my head saying, *"Is this all there is?"* to finding myself in the bomb shelter of the kibbutz I lived on in the Golan Heights in Israel, writing my goodbyes to those I loved having been warned of an imminent chemical weapons attack by the Syrians. I've been in several car accidents with my parents where my life flashed before me but when I had two near-death incidences, one so soon after the other, it provoked me to take a step that I would not have otherwise taken.

The first car accident was in late September, 2011 on Route 2 on the way to Walden Pond in Concord, Massachusetts for a swim, and the second was close on its heels on one of the main roads in the town we live in, Marblehead, Mass. in early January, 2012.

The First Car Accident was Ground-shifting

We were driving in the left-hand lane when the cars in front of us suddenly began to swerve erratically. Blane was busy dealing with the swerving cars but was unable to avoid the construction material that had fallen off a truck ahead of us. Our tire caught the end of a long metal pipe and flipped it so that it harpooned the window and, in slow motion, flew directly at my heart. During what felt like minutes that the pipe hurtled towards me, the three options in my future flashed in front of me: I would survive physically unscathed, die, or be gravely wounded or disabled.

As the safety mesh within the window glass caught the pipe, stopping its final penetration inches from my chest, I was violently showered by an unknown fluid. It was as if a large cup of liquid had been thrown angrily, directly at my face, and it seemed to come from the pipe. Like a crazy person, I began to wipe it off, believing it was something toxic that would start to make my skin crawl, whither, and peel off.

As Blane pulled off at the next exit, he calmly reassured me that this liquid had not come from the pipe but from the water bottle I had been holding. With the shock of the impact it had abruptly emptied its contents over me.

When we were finally able to pull over and the car stopped, I realized I was covered from head to toe with fine bits of glass, but other than that I was physically unharmed.

Long after this accident, my heart felt energetically penetrated, like there was a hole, a hollow void in my chest that penetrated deep into my soul.

I had started writing this book at the beginning of that year. After this incident, I wrote with a vengeance, believing that I was being told to complete this project and that if I didn't, my life would be taken from me. I felt I was hovering on the edge between life and death. There was no solid ground beneath me, no sense of clarity; I was just faithfully following blindly, doing what I was being told to do.

I became a slave to my writing, often writing many hours day and night, but even so, I loved writing, how it focused me on expressing what I had learned.

By the beginning of 2012, I had finished my book and given it to five friends to read for feedback. Blane and I had scheduled an impromptu vacation in the Dominican Republic and I estimated that by the time we returned, I would have my feedback and move into editing.

The Second Car Accident Came Out of Nowhere

A week before our vacation, after work one Sunday, a 16-year old who was driving his mother's SUV at about 40 mph the wrong way down a side street barreled through the intersection and hit my side of the car, the passenger side. In the micro seconds before the impact, I saw the car, the driver, and its three occupants. The sound of the impact was huge, like an explosion. My body whipped violently from side to side and a pain shot through my neck. Just as in the previous accident, my thoughts quickly scanned through all three possible outcomes.

Blane and I emerged with severe cases of whiplash, and neither of us could work in the months that followed. We were forced to accept a slower pace of life, which focused on recuperation.

A week later, we were on our way to the Dominican Republic, looking forward to the sun and sea. How could that not help heal our ailing bodies? But the trip was a disaster; if ever there was a prize for the worst vacation, this one would be in the running for first place.

We returned from our vacation needing a vacation, wondering *what it was all about*. Hadn't I been doing what I was supposed to be doing? So why was I so abruptly and violently shaken up and nearly killed by two projectiles, first a harpoon and then a car? I felt lost and aimless. It didn't occur to me that these incidents were a matter of chance. I just didn't believe that. I knew, **we** knew, there was meaning to be had, but we simply couldn't find it. Clients and friends would say, "Well you're obviously being told something. What is it?" It was so clear we were being told to pay attention, to change something, but we didn't know what to pay attention to or what to change.

The Channel with a Vision

Not long after the first accident, a local bodyworker had mentioned a friend of hers who was a channel, and instinctively I knew I should book a session with her. After this second incident, I *had* to call her and set up the meeting. Seeing that Blane had been the driver in both of these accidents, and knowing without any doubt that our destinies were headed into the future together, we went to our appointment with the channel together. Neither of us had ever been to a channel before.

Hello dear ones, Monique & Blane. We have come from far away to speak to you. It is the preparation you have done in waiting for this session that has allowed us to come through and we thank you for your open presence.

There has been a long waiting game. We have been calling to you. You have had a sense that there is information waiting and we are grateful for your audience tonight.

Before we go on, I see a woman, a mother, she has an anxious manner about her and reddish, brown hair. She's very forceful, she's saying, "This is my turn, I want to be here." There's a sense of urgency she always had, agitation. She's your mother Monique, because she's saying, "That's my daughter." She's so urgent and she has a high level of anxiety. She's so anxious she's getting in her own way of giving me the message. It's like she's shaking you because she wants you to pay attention. She's shaking you so pennies will come out. Now she's showing me an arm. Did you hurt your arm? She's showing me your arm saying, "Why did it have to get to this point to get you to pay attention?" We continue to get things that stop us until we stop.

There's something literary about you. You've known it, that there's something you've had to express and you haven't been expressing it through writing. She's showing me your arm and that you've been shaken for a reason. She's showing me, almost like a piggy bank that you shake the pennies out of. Then she's showing me how you're supposed to help children, that something will come from you if you listen and it will help children, a lot of children.

She's watching everything and it's very hard for her to be so impotent. It's hard from her vantage point because she wants you to have figured this out by now. I think she's a fairly impatient person and a little frazzled. She's saying it's not too late, you'll get there when you get there. She's self-soothing, she's calming down, which is nice. It's unusual to have a spirit that is so agitated but she said she needed to come in a form you knew her. Now she's saying she's going to resume and she's moved closer to me.

I would like to speak to you about your career. There are forms that a life takes, it is complicated, it is complex but it is also beautifully woven. You have the opportunity to take a turn in your life, and to touch more people than you are touching, and this is what I was trying to indicate with the shake. It is important to expand your reach, to be accessible to more people and it cannot happen in your current form of work. We ask you to articulate, to write, to share, to lead groups, to move out into the public domain: it will depend less on your hands and more on your abilities as an intuitive healer.

They're saying you already know your message, what it would be. They say you will spend more time on your message than on your private work. They say you have a method that you could teach other people, and that it could develop in people and that it could spread across the country. Is doesn't mean that your daily life has to implode or explode or do anything drastic, but your inner world would expand. You might still see some private clients, but you would minimize that in order to expand your work. If you do that your daily life would go more smoothly and you wouldn't have so many surprises and shocks. It's been a wake-up call for you lately.

They want me to talk about 'magnitude'. You feel sometimes small, and that you are in a small pond currently, but you have the potential to be very big. You have a sense of that but you see it as hubris or ego so you don't always let yourself address it. But what happens is like an ant on top of a volcano, and if you feel small and your power is that big, it's starts to rumble and things start to happen, until you realize, "Oh, I have a volcano's amount of explosive power inside of me." Once you see that, it explodes in a good direction and the reverberations are like money falls from the sky and good things come your way and it opens up lots of positive experiences.

Your mother is saying thank you to me. She really loves you. She's telling me you're a good person.

Life is full of pregnant possibilities. You are at a crossroads, there are decisions to be made. We feel you need our guidance and that is why we have scheduled this visit with you. We have been called specifically because we see the bigger picture. It is difficult when you have lives on earth to see everything, the evolution of what is to come but also where you have been and what is expected in these lifetimes so we are here to offer our love, our compassion, our devotion and specifically our advice, if you are willing to hear it and to listen as we feel you are.

This is an exciting time for you, and that's what we want to say more than anything else. It's a time of development, of freedom and of encouraging further and further growth. You will talk about this night as a turning point when you look back. You will teach the importance of listening to spirit, and you will show the difference of just putting your hands on someone and aligning yourself with spirit and allowing spirit to do the work with you, and the difference in the results.

This is not a scary time. You may have interpreted some of the things that are happening as a call for attention, but you are giving it attention and you have been doing the best you can to deal with the things that have come before you. You do not have to be afraid— you are listening. There are good things ahead. You must go on your individual pathways with a vengeance: explore, explode and you will feel free and the greyness will lift and life will again feel pleasurable and light and carefree.

Monique, it is very important that you write, as briefly and concisely as possible, what you would teach, what crystalizes your approach and your goals. You will sit down and say, "What is the synthesis, what have I done, what are the important aspects and motives to this body of work I have developed?" You would then get that into as concise a form as possible and start to move out into the world and find out what that is like. This can only happen if you simplify your life and stay where you are and work on these goals for a while until the fountain of information starts to spurt and you start to understand our words. It feels like it will be a hard thing to do, but once you start you will find, "Oh my goodness, I do have a body of work that needs to be expressed." These incidences you have been experiencing are the product of the world trying to stop you in your tracks and get you to listen to what must happen **now** in order for it to happen at all.

It's an auspicious time. Once you fulfill these obligations to yourself and you express yourself with integrity to the public in a way that revitalizes you, you will find that you are in more and more demand.

Those two incidences are to inform your work, they are part of the story of what you'll be teaching, they add to the body of knowledge that you have and will make your work more profound and palatable to people because those stories will be your introduction to what brought you to write this, which they're saying people find compelling, when they see that someone's life took a turn because of dramatic circumstances.

They're saying those incidences are not even the wake up calls. They're showing me that in our culture those would be the two wake-up calls but if you look deeply into what's been moving you, it's more of an internal feeling of, "Is this all there is?" That's the wake-up call. If you're heading in the direction that spirit is calling you, you won't feel that, ever. If you do, it will tell you that you're not listening. That's what they're saying is the wake-up call.

Your job here on earth is to bring healing and calm. We expect you to do that on a grander scheme. For if you would just listen to your body's callings and your psychic leanings you would see yourself expanding from this town to a much bigger audience.

It's important that you reach out to children. You're here to help change peoples consciousness. You will find that children respond even more quickly than adults to your interventions. Children don't vibrate in a synchronistic fashion with you. When you are in their presence in your newest form and you are attempting to impart your wisdom to a group of people you will find your work will necessarily have to be with children, because it will help them so much. You will feel compelled to reach out to the younger generation: it will give you more hope.

Partnering on the Dual Path

People often comment on how much time Blane and I spend together, because we're almost always together. They also comment on how often they see us hold hands. We were not present for each other's childhoods, missed the opportunity to bring each other laughter, joy, wisdom or the warmth of our heart when we needed it most. Life teaches us that missed experiences can never be fully shared.

Partnering is a challenge to the soul and spirit to which many do not rise. Most people are in a relationship, seeking one, ending one or believing they can never have one. Despite the call of our hearts for love, the multi-dimensionality of relationships mirrors and magnifies the multi-dimensionality and complexity of each one of us. Having answered the call of our heart, we rest our head and body in the softness of our love and only full awaken again when there is strife within or around us.

Partnering is two people, each one committed to their own journey and each deciding to take that journey together.

The Partnering Journey

Blane and I share books, reading to one another on road trips and often in bed before going to sleep. We often show each other clothing, books, magazines and art we are interested in, flowers that look or smell good, a beautiful section of sky, clouds that evoke our imagination. We make each other meals, talk, and contemplate together. We go for walks together, hand in hand. We meditate and do our Qigong practices alone, and sometimes go for walks alone, read alone, eat alone and contemplate alone. Together and alone we work, sleep, laugh, play, struggle and explore.

Being with each other, in love, enjoying each other's company, is not a *stage* in a relationship, it *is* a relationship.

Because common wisdom says that if we spend too much time together we'll get bored with each other and we'll lose the mystery and magic, many relationships are only a succession of dinner engagements, a time to catch up on what the other missed (which can never truly be expressed).

The magic and the mystery in a relationship is that it reveals and displays all of who we are, particularly the aspects we try to hide from ourselves. Just the thought of this can make us avoid a relationship altogether, but the right relationship also provides us with a best friend, the person we most trust, respect and honor, the love and support we need, and a much needed place of rest and sanctuary.

There's no better way to tackle our demons. It's better than keeping them under lock and key. Demons are notorious for picking locks and showing up when we least want them to, ruining a night's sleep, a birthday party or a day off. Why not spend that sleepless night, once the winds have settled, sifting through the debris together?

When first we meet and get to know someone, we often begin by presenting the best of ourselves. We tend to make ourselves look our best (hands, hair and clothing all well-manicured); we're on our best behavior, charming and funny, careful not to drink too much, swear too much or eat too much. This 'best' is a thin and pretentious layer of who we are.

As the relationship moves along its natural course, we make discoveries about ourselves and our partners; complications arise in our interactions and communication, emotions and reactions spiral out of control until we come face to face with the worst, rather than the best. Below the well-groomed surface, a whole new world may be revealed: anger, jealousy, laziness, depression, non-communication, withdrawal of affection, issues of control, addictive behavior…

This worst part of ourselves is a conglomeration of our past: our pains, experiences, reactions, and behavior we have been exposed to. The worst part of ourselves, the demon within, the disruptions in our energetic matrix, holds the key to our growth and can be our most profound teacher.

We have been taught that to love is to accept each other as we are; the good with the bad. This level of acceptance leads to nothing but a lifetime of struggle between the thinly veiled layer of 'best' and the 'monster within.'

There are many kinds of relationship, but one with an intact spirit and soul is where each person is engaged in their own deepening and unraveling, and is fully present for that of the other. There is no circumstance where one person is the 'healthy one' and the other is the one who needs 'help;' this language and thought-process is all wrong. A relationship is a puzzle, and part of the journey is to discover how pieces that are constantly in flux, fit and move together.

Since ultimately we are individuals, much of this work can and should be done alone, but a relationship brings with it uncharted ground that changes when we least expect it to and its earthquake-like movements heave up fertile soil for us to work with.

To do this work within a relationship, there must be a dedication, a sense of security, love and acceptance.

Dedication to self-growth, wisdom and maturity, and to continually returning to the lesson.

Sense of security from knowing we have the freedom to choose to be here or not. Love is a given, but partnering is not. We choose each other *because* we are on this path, because we delight in being witness to each other's growth and discoveries.

Love of the journey, discovery and growth; our own and that of our beloved.

Acceptance of this leg of the journey and that there will most-likely be another ahead.

Both similarities and differences draw us into relationship with our chosen partner.

Similarities often create a sense of connection and harmony, while differences often create dissonance. There is strength and wisdom for us in both. In many relationships there is one who is laid back while the other is driven (In the typical American heterosexual relationship, it is often the female who is driven and the male laid back), and there we remain polarized and fixed in stone, in comparison our identities seemingly made clearer.

Our tool box needs to be full—we all need to know when and how to turn the engine off and back on again.

This journey is about opening and expanding to the heavens; a relationship is a second engine moving you along your path. Within a relationship that connects the soul of two people, trouble, misunderstandings, irritation, anger (as long as it's not abusive), can be fuel for the engine, driving you to look in, back, and around for perspective and understanding.

Remember, that although a relationship can be a second engine that propels you forward, it is *you* who is the primary source of energy on this journey, *you* who brings dedication. Also remember, it is you who is on the journey, and the relationship that is along for the ride. It has to be this way; *you* are and always will be the only constant in *your* life.

Resources: *The Secret to Desire in a Long-Term Relationship* by Esther Perel on Ted.com

Blane and Monique

Blane says he remembers the day we met distinctly. I was outdoors working on my motorcycle, a Honda Rebel, hand-painting the gas tank. "Is that your bike?" he asked. He remembers he had his Carhartt jacket on and I was wearing a yellow t-shirt; my hair was long and all crazy, and another guy from his martial arts class had just tried to hit on me. Blane told me he used to do drawings for people to put on their cars. It was a sunny autumn day and Blane was wearing a bandana and carrying a staff.

It was around 1990 when his martial arts school moved into Rugg Road, the artist building I was living and working in. One of my co-workers at Model Mugging (a national self-defense program) had told me that a martial arts school was looking for a new space, and I suggested they sub-lease from the martial arts school that was down the hall from me. Blane and I met, and an easy friendship formed, with us going out for an occasional lunch or my inviting him in for a hearty miso soup.

I found Blane to be smart, insightful, thoughtful and funny. Although I found him *so* very attractive in *so* many ways, in my experience there was no actual correlation between attractiveness and a relationship working out, *and* he was married. Hence the friendship—during which, for many years, Blane was under the assumption that I was gay.

Some years later, we met up again by chance at Harnett's, a wonderful little store in Harvard Square that has since closed. We talked for a while and I invited him to my Kali class (Indonesian stick fighting) that evening. It was a bitterly cold night in Blue Hills and once the class was over I realized I'd locked my keys in the car. As we all tried to break into the car, Blane offered me his jacket. I had become a 'strong independent woman' and didn't need some man coddling me or thinking I couldn't take care of myself. In fact, his offering felt like an embarrassment in front of the all-male class I had worked to become accepted by. However, I was freezing and after some insistence on his part, I gave in and put on his wonderfully warm jacket. This struggle to soften, to accept help and take shelter when offered was to follow me into our relationship.

It was still some time before Blane called me to let me know he was getting divorced, was really stressed out, and needed a massage.

His marriage had been in trouble for many years, and he'd just come to the end of the five years he'd given it to improve. During those five years he had worked hard on his marriage and was now tired and worn. Knowing that Blane was also a Massage Therapist, I suggested that we do an exchange—if he were my client, rather than friends doing an exchange, we would always be friends and nothing more, and I sensed there was the potential for more. We did our first exchange and started to spend and enjoy time with each other again. We'd spend our lunches talking, going for long walks by the river, and occasionally going to martial arts classes together.

On the heels of the end of his marriage, it was a bittersweet time. My divorce had happened quite some years previous and I was in a stable, settled and clear place to be a support for him as he worked through the events of his marriage, choices each of them had made, his memories and grief.

It is said that there are more than two people in a relationship, what with parents, siblings, ex's... Our past comes along for the ride, burdening us with its influence on our decisions, emotions and needs. As time went on, the past we still carried with us showed up more and more frequently, and our ability to have a relationship free from anger and distrust became a real challenge.

I believe most couples at this point, stop challenging themselves and growing as individuals. When this happens couples often become polarized and a sense of rivalry develops as they enter into a relationship based on competition.

For partnership to succeed, a soul decision needs to be made, and this soul decision can only be made if you are soul mates. For us, our soul decision was obvious; we had a deep sense of *knowing* that being together was right, and a powerful sense of kinship. We knew we were animals of the same kind, spirits that were meant to find each other and walk this Earth, for however long, together.

Having made this decision, we could move forward together, protecting each other's back, paving the way forward and helping to heal the wounds that surfaced.

At various junctures in any relationship there are challenges and difficult choices to be faced. We quite simply and profoundly chose trust rather than distrust, and as we did, our enormous respect for each other created an environment where we could reflect each other in ways that brought our personal pains and dynamics to the full light of day where we could look at them, and again make a choice—to continue carrying our destructive burdens with us or to begin to let go, move forward and transform.

Making the choice to let go, move forward and transform is not easy. New choices must be repeated again and again, until the tracks we have worn in the road of our psyche changes and the going suddenly becomes smoother and less obstructed. Since that time long ago, when we first made our choice, we have step-by-step, been uncovering the hidden depths with trust, care and gentleness, and sometimes with the power and energy of the shifting of tectonic plates.

Blane is my sunlight, my Earth, my Heaven and the glow in my heart. And if we one day part, for whatever reason, along with all that goes with it, will be the time and space to learn, grow and understand. Until then, our souls dance this life together, entwined in the delicate hold of gracious beauty.

Partnering on the Dual Path: A Love Story

Thanking My Tribe

My tribe is made up of people I know and those I have never met, the living and the long-gone; those who have taken steps towards awakening their spirit. I have quoted some of them in this book, and whenever possible, I have included photos of them to emphasize that they are ordinary folk who are extraordinary in that they have had the courage to make deep internal shifts, to transform their internal world and the world we live in.

Blane, my love, friend, and soul mate.

Friends and clients with whom discoveries and journeys have been shared.

Hugh Milne, for your amazing teachings over the years.

The lineage of Xiantianwujimen for agreeing to share the sacred and profound lineage of Qigong.

My designer, Nancy Wolinski, who has always done the most amazing work for us and who has created a masterpiece with the design on this book, and my editor, Laura Smith, for taking on this project because it *spoke to her* and for doing such an excellent job.

Everyone and anyone who has sowed the seed of forward movement and inward sight. This is my tribe, scattered like seeds in the wind. Each of us following our hearts and awakening our spirits, slowly transforming ourselves and everyone we touch.

An enormous thanks to all 88 of my Indiegogo Backers. Your support brightens my spirit. A full list of Backers can be found on our website and a special thank you to the following: Alex and Nora Falk, Jeff and Laurie Flowers, Aimee Mullins, and Christina Pastan.

Reading and Reference List

Rather than order this list by category and risk the reader only going to the category they believe they need or are interested in, it is alphabetical by book name to encourage the opportunity of discovery.

A

The Adonis Complex: The Secret Crisis of Male Body Obsession by Harrison Pope, Katherine Phillips and Roberto Olivardia

Anam Cara: A Book of Celtic Wisdom by John O'Donohue

Apartment Composting by Mark Cullen, Lorraine Johnson and Andrew Leyerle

The Art of Being and Becoming by Hazrat Inayat Khan

Atlas of Anatomy by Anne Gilroy

Awakening the Heroes Within by Carol Pearson

B

Baby Not on Board: A Celebration of Life without Kids by Jennifer Shawne

Beauty by John O'Donohue (also available on CD. Highly recommended)

Be Here Now by Ram Dass

Beyond Antibiotics by Keith Sehner, MD and Lendon Smith, M.D.

Beyond Stillness by Charles Ridley

Bitter Fruit: Women's Experiences of Unplanned Pregnancy, Abortion and Adoption by Rita Townsend and Ann Perkins

The Bodies Many Cries for Water by Fereydoon Batmanghelidj, M.D.

The Body Moveable by David Gorman

The Bone People by Kerri Hulme

Breasts: A Natural and Unnatural History by Florence Williams

Breath, Mind and Consciousness by Harish Johari

Buddha by Karen Armstrong

Buddha at Bedtime: Tales of Love and Wisdom for You to Read with Your Child to Enchant, Enlighten and Inspire by Dharmachari Nagaraja.

C

D

E

Eat, Pray, Love by Elizabeth Gilbert

The Element: how Finding Your Passion Changes Everything by Ken Robinson, Ph.D.

Emotional Anatomy: The Structure of Experience by Stanley Keleman, Center Press, centerpress.com

Energy Exercises for Health and Vitality by John Chitty and Mary Muller

Everything You Always Wanted to Ask Your Gynecologist by Scott Thornton and Kathleen Schramm

Exposed: The Toxic Chemistry of Everyday Products and What's at Stake for American Power by Mark Schapiro

F

Facing the Dragon: Confronting Personal and Spiritual Grandiosity by Robert Moore

Family Energetics by Deborah Donndelinger

Fast Food Nation: The Dark Side of the All-American Meal by Eric Schlosser

The Field: The Quest for the Secret Force of the Universe by Lynne McTaggart

Finding Your Element: How to Discover Your Talents and Passion and Transform Your Life by Ken Robinson, Ph.D.

Fire in the Belly: On Being a Man by Sam Keen

The Flowering of Human Consciousness by Eckhart Tolle

Fountain of Youth Exercises: For Vitality, Radiance, Joy and Fulfillment in Fifteen Minutes by Naomi Sophia Call © 2011, published by Findhorn Press, Scotland

Four Arguments for the Elimination of Television by Jerry Mander

G

The Genie in Your Genes by Dawson Church

Get It Off! Understanding the Cause of Breast Pain, Cysts and Cancer by Sydney Singer and Soma Grismaijer

The Gift of Fear by Gavin de Becker

The Good Men Project: Real Stories from the Front Lines of Modern Manhood by Tom Matlack and Larry Bean

The Great Transformation: The Beginning of Our Religious Traditions by Karen Armstrong

Grow Great Grub: Organic Food for Small Spaces by Gayla Trail

Growing Old is Not for Sissies by Etta Clark

O

The Orient in the Mirror by Roland and Sabrina Michaud

Original Self: Living with Paradox and Originality by Thomas Moore

Organic Gardening Beginners Manual by Julie Turner

The Organic Lawn Care Manual: A Natural, Low-Maintenance System for a Beautiful, Safe Lawn by Paul Tukey

Overtreated: Why Too Much Medicine is Making Us Sicker and Poorer by Shannon Brownlee

P

A Path with Heart: A Guide Through the Perils and Promises of Spiritual Life by Jack Kornfield

Planting Seeds: Practicing Mindfulness with Children by Thich Nhat Hanh

Plastic: A Toxic Love Story by Susan Freinkel

Plastic-Free: How I Kicked the Plastic Habit and How You Can Too by Beth Terry

Platero and I by Juan Ramon Jimenez

The Plug-In Drug: Television, Computers, and Family Life by Marie Winn

The Polarity Process by Franklyn Sills, North Atlantic Books

Polarity Therapy Volumes 1 and 2 by Dr. Randolph Stone

The Power of Now by Eckhart Tolle

Power Up Your Brain: The Neuroscience of Enlightenment by David Perlmutter, M.D. and Alberto Villoldo, Ph.D. Copyright 2011, Hay House Inc., Carlsbad, CA.

The Price of Motherhood: Why the Most Important Job in the World Is Still the Least Valued by Ann Crittenden

Protecting the Gift by Gavin de Becker

The Prophet by Kahlil Gibran

Pushed: The Painful Truth about Childbirth and Modern Maternity Care by Jennifer Block

R

The Raw Transformation: Energizing Your Life with Living Foods by Wendy Rudell

Real Boys by William Pollack

Real Boys' Voices by William Pollack

Real Food Has Curves: How to Get Off Processed Foods, Lose Weight and Love What You Eat by Bruce Weinstein and Mark Scarbrough

Remotely Controlled: How Television is Damaging our Lives by Aric Sigman

U

Uninformed Consent: The Hidden Dangers in Dental Care by Hal Huggins

The Urban/Suburban Composter: The Complete Guide to Backyard, Balcony and Apartment Composting by Mark Cullen, Lorraine Johnson and Andrew Leyerle

V

Vibrational Medicine by Richard Gerber, M.D.

W

When Healing Becomes a Crime: The Amazing Story of the Hoxsey Cancer Clinics and the Return of Alternative Therapies by Kenny Ausubel

Whole Body Dentistry by Mark Breiner

Wisdom in the Body by Michael Kern

Working on Yourself Alone by Arnold Mindell

Working with Anger by Thubten Chodron

Why Your Life Sucks and What You Can Do About It by Alan Cohen

Y

You: The Owner's Manual by Michael Roizen

You: The Smart Patient by Michael Roizen

Younger Next Year: A Guide to Living Like 50 Until You're 80 and Beyond by Chris Crowley and Henry Lodge, M.D.

Your Body Speaks its Mind by Stanley Keleman

Z

Zen: The Supreme Experience by Alan and Mark Watts

Zen and the Art of Making a Living by Laurence Boldt

10 Principles for Spiritual Parenting: Nurturing Your Child's Soul by Mimi Doe

Online Resources and Inspirations

Online Articles and Webcasts

Antibiotics May Make Fighting Flu Harder, by Tina Hesman Saey in Science News article. http://www. sciencenews.org/view/generic/id/71187/description/Antibiotics_may_make_fighting_flu_ harder

Holocaust survivors 3 times more likely to attempt suicide by Tamara Traubmann, Haaretz Correspondent. http://www.haaretz.com/news/study-holocaust-survivors-3-times-more-likely-to-attempt-suicide-1.166386

How Antibiotics Destroy Your Immune System by Craig Stellpflug in Natural News article, http://www. naturalnews.com/036479_antibiotics_immune_system_destruction.html

Inner Peace: We Yearn for Silence, Yet, the Less Sound there is, the More our Thoughts Deafen Us. How Can we Still the Noise Within? by Tim Parks in Aeon Magazine: http://www.aeonmagazine.com/altered-states/is-the-sound-of-silence-the-end-of-the-self/

New Study Reveals That Antibiotics Damage Our Immune System by Heidi Stevenson in Gaia Health article: http://www. gaia-health.com/articles401/000445-antibiotics-damage-immune-system.shtml

Newtown Author's Book Helps Those Affected by Shootings by Sandra Diamond Fox: http://www.ctpost.com/local/article/Newtown-author-s-book-helps-those-affected-by-4548793.php

Restoring the Body: Bessel van der Kolk on Yoga, EMDR, and Treating Trauma at: http://www.onbeing.org/program/restoring-the-body-bessel-van-der-kolk-on-yoga-emdr-and-treating-trauma/5801#sthash.f9H81H7f.dpuf

Ted.com

These links can be found on the links page on www.adualpath.com and are continually updated.

All it Takes is 10 Mindful Minutes – Andy Puddicombe

Changing My Legs and My Mindset – Aimee Mullins (also on aimeemullins.com)

The Council of Dads – Bruce Feller

The Danger of a Single Story – Chimamanda Adichie

Epigenetics and the Space Around Us – Dr. Paul Brenner

The Happy Secret to Better Work – Shawn Achor

Healing through Diet – Dean Ornish

The Hidden Power of Smiling – Ron Gutman

My 12 Pairs of Legs – Aimee Mullins (also on aimeemullins.com)

Listening to Shame – Brené Brown (also on Brenebrown.com)

The Opportunity for Adversity – Aimee Mullins (also on aimeemullins.com)

The Power of Vulnerablity – Brené Brown (also on Brenebrown.com)

The Secret to Desire in a Long-Term Relationship – Esther Perel

The Surprising Science of Happiness – Dan Gilbert

Teach Every Child About Food – Jamie Oliver

To This Day…For the Bullied and the Beautiful – Shane Koycan

Try Something New for 30 Days – Matt Cutts

What Adults Can Learn from Kids – Adora Svitak

Why You Will Fail to Have a Great Career – Larry Smith

Other Web Resources

Aeonmagazine.com

Aquasana.com

Daoist-qigong.com

Ewg.org: Skin Deep

Endangeredearth.com

Gratefulness.org

IUCN.org (International Union for Conservation of Nature)

Myplasticfreelife.com

Lifewithoutplastic.com

Onbeing.org

Soundstrue.com

Spiritualityhealth.com

Sproutpeople.org

Thecouncilofdads.com

Zenhabits.net

Movies and Documentaries

America the Beautiful

A documentary that examines America's fixation with outward appearance and the unrealistic standards of beauty dictated by the media, pop culture and the fashion industry. Featuring interviews with fashion experts, media personalities and celebrities, the film looks at everything from plastic surgery's growing popularity to widespread concerns about eating disorders.

America the Beautiful: 2

A documentary that looks at how the national obsession with weight loss has negatively affected our perception of what really constitutes a healthy weight.

Blue Gold

Wars of the future will be fought over water as they are over oil today, as the source of human survival enters the global marketplace and political arena. Corporate giants, private investors, and corrupt governments vie for control of our dwindling supply, prompting protests, lawsuits, and revolutions from citizens fighting for the right to survive.

Chemerical

Follows an american family as they attempt to rid their home of toxic substances. It explores the life cycle of everyday household cleaners and hygiene products to prove that, thanks to our clean obsession, we are drowning in a sea of toxicity.

Carbon Nation

An optimistic, solutions-based, non-preachy film that shows tackling climate change boosts the economy, increases national security and promotes health and a clean environment.

David vs. Monsanto

Imagine that a storm blows across your garden—and that now, without your knowledge and without your consent, foreign and genetically-manipulated seeds are in your vegetable patch which you have nourished and maintained for over 50 years. A few days later, representatives of a large multi-national corporation secretly visit your home, only to return later and demand that you surrender all your vegetables and seeds. Then, they file a lawsuit against you for the illegal use of patented and genetically-modified seeds that you never planted or used and, what's more—the court rules in favor of the corporation! Yet, you still fight back…

Dirt

A look at man's relationship with Dirt. We started our journey together as stardust, swirled by cosmic forces into our galaxy, solar system, and planet. We are made of the same stuff.

Doctored

A documentary on the monopolization of our medical system reveals an alarming portrait of deception and criminality.

Cut, Poison, Burn

A documentary that puts the business of cancer treatment under the microscope. Follow the frustrating journeys of critically ill cancer patients as they try to navigate the confusing and dangerous maze of treatment and encounter formidable obstacles in the "cancer industrial complex."

Farmaggedon

The story of family farms that were providing healthy foods to their communities and were forced to stop by agents of misguided government bureaucracies.

Fat, Sick and Nearly Dead

Chronicles one man's personal mission to regain his health while traveling across US, juicer in tow, and inspiring others to do the same.

Finding Joe

In the early 20th century while studying world mythology, Joseph Campbell discovered a pattern hidden in every story ever told. He called it "the hero's journey." Finding Joe explores how the hero's journey is relevant and essential in today's world.

Flow

An award-winning documentary investigation into what experts label the most important political and environmental issue of the 21st Century—The World Water Crisis.

The Flowering of Human Consciousness

Eckhart Tolle is known worldwide for his teaching about spiritual enlightenment through the power of the present moment. On this DVD, viewers come face-to-face with Tolle for a transformational meeting with the respected teacher.

Food Beware

Follows an experiment in a small village in the mountains of France, where—in opposition to powerful economic interests—the town's mayor has decided to make the school lunch menu organic, with much of it grown locally.

Food, Inc.

Exposes how our nation's food supply is controlled by a handful of corporations that often put profit ahead of consumer health, the livelihood of the American farmer, the safety of workers and our own environment.

Food Matters

With nutritionally-depleted foods, chemical additives and our tendency to rely upon pharmaceutical drugs to treat what's wrong with our malnourished bodies, it's no wonder that modern society is getting sicker. Food Matters sets about uncovering the trillion dollar worldwide sickness industry and gives people some scientifically verifiable solutions for overcoming illness naturally. The message of this documentary film, "Let thy Food be thy Medicine and thy Medicine be thy Food" —Hippocrates.

Forks Over Knives

Examines the profound claim that most; if not all; of the so-called "diseases of affluence" that afflict us can be controlled; or even reversed; by rejecting our present menu of animal-based and processed foods.

Fresh

Outlines the vicious cycle of our current food production methods, while also celebrating the farmers, thinkers and business people across America who are reinventing our food system.

Happy

Takes us on a journey from the swamps of Louisiana to the slums of Kolkata in search of what really makes people happy. Combining real life stories of people from around the world and powerful interviews with the leading scientists in happiness research, HAPPY explores the secrets behind our most valued emotion.

Head Games

A documentary on one of leading public health issues of our time: head injuries in sports.

Hungry for Change

Exposes secrets the diet, weight loss and food industries don't want you to know about deceptive strategies designed to keep you coming back for more.

I am

The story of a successful Hollywood director, Tom Shadyac, who experienced a life threatening head injury, and his ensuing journey to try and answer two very basic questions: What s wrong with our world? and What can we do about it? Tom visits some of today s great minds, including authors, poets, teachers, religious leaders, and scientists searching for the fundamental endemic problem that causes all of the other problems, while simultaneously reflecting on this own life choices of excess, greed and eventual healing. *"We started by asking what s wrong wit the world, and ended up discovering what s right with it."* —Tom Shadyac

King Corn

Engrossing and eye-opening, a fun and crusading journey into the digestive tract of our fast food nation where one ultra-industrial, pesticide-laden, heavily-subsidized commodity dominates the food pyramid from top to bottom—corn.

Last Call at the Oasis

Water. It's the earth's most valuable resource. Our cities are powered by it, countless industries depend on it, and all living things need it to survive. But it's very possible that in the near future, there won't be enough to sustain life on our planet.

May I be Frank

Frank Ferrante is a 54 year-old Sicilian from Brooklyn living in San Francisco. A lover of life, great food, beautiful women and a good laugh, Frank is also a drug addict, morbidly obese, pre-diabetic, and fighting Hepatitis C. May I Be Frank documents the transformation of Frank's life.

Mercury Undercover

The dangers of mercury exposing the cause and effect of the well-hidden evidence of mercury contamination as seen through the eyes of doctors, scientists, environmental experts and mercury-poisoned survivors.

Plastic Planet

A journey around the globe to reveal the far-flung reach of plastic. Interviews with the world's foremost experts shed light on the perils of plastic to our environment and expose the truth of how plastic affects our bodies...and the health of future generations.

Processed People

Processed People examines these topics: Why are we so fat? What is health? Health care or sick care? Are we what we eat? Do we need to eat animal products? What's the role of exercise? What's a processed person? Can you 'de-process' yourself? What happens if we don't change?

Simply Raw: Reversing Diabetes in 30 Days

An independent documentary film that chronicles six Americans with diabetes (one with Type 1) who switch to a diet consisting entirely of vegan, organic, uncooked food in order to reverse disease without pharmaceutical medication.

Super Size Me

While examining the influence of the fast food industry, Morgan Spurlock personally explores the consequences on his health of a diet of solely McDonald's food for one month.

Switch

What will it really take, to go from the energy that built our world, to the energy that will shape our future?

Tapped

A behind-the-scenes look into the unregulated and unseen world of an industry that aims to privatize and sell back the one resource that ought never to become a commodity: our water.

Trashed

Looks at the risks to the food chain and the environment through pollution of our air, land and sea by waste. The film reveals surprising truths about very immediate and potent dangers to our health.

Vegucated

A guerrilla-style documentary that follows three meat—and cheese-loving New Yorkers who agree to adopt a vegan diet for six weeks and learn what it's all about.

Visit www.adualpath.com for more resources, to purchase the Sacred Bodywork DVD, download individual techniques, do online tutoring, or to register for a more in-depth program.

Always have
compassion
in your heart

Always have
compassion
in your heart